LATIN PROVERBS

LATIN PROVERBS

WISDOM FROM ANCIENT TO MODERN TIMES

WALDO E. SWEET

Bolchazy-Carducci Publishers, Inc.
Wauconda, Illinois USA

Contributing Editors
Georgia Irby-Massie
Scott Van Horn

Latin Proverbs

Bolchazy-Carducci Publishers, Inc.
1000 Brown Street
Wauconda, IL 60084 USA
www.bolchazy.com

Printed in the United States of America
2005
by United Graphics

ISBN-13: 978-0-86516-544-1
ISBN-10: 0-86516-544-0

Library of Congress Cataloging-in-Publication Data

Latin proverbs : wisdom from ancient to modern times : c. 100 various
authors, ancient to contemporary / collected and adapted from Waldo E.
Sweet's Artes Latinae series.
   p. cm.
 ISBN 0-86516-544-0 (pbk.)
 1. Proverbs, Latin. 2. Proverbs, Latin--Translations into English.
I. Sweet, Waldo E.

PN6418 .L37 2002
398.9'71--dc21

            2002012846

Contents

Introduction

This book is a treasure trove of ancient and contemporary wisdom, offering 1,188 dual-language quotations for enlightenment, amusement, and for use on special occasions. Amaze your friends, impress your colleagues, surprise your family! Find just the right sentiment or nugget of wisdom in this collection of Latin quotations, complete with English translations. Approximately one hundred authors, ancient to contemporary, are represented, as well as quotations from the Bible, state and institutional mottoes, and legal phrases.

The quotations are by turns advisory ("Life should be used; for life slips by on rapid feet"), admonitory ("Drunkenness takes away your character, your money, and your reputation"), philosophical ("Contemplation of nature is food for the mind"), folksy ("Good friends appear in difficulties"), intriguing ("Heaven itself is sought through foolishness"), pithy ("Enough eloquence, little wisdom"), ironic ("Conquered Greece captured her savage victor"), and striking ("What no one knows almost does not occur"). There are commonplaces ("Time diminishes grief") and their quirky predecessors ("The cowl does not make the monk"). Browse through them for inspiration, or just for fun.

Whimsical black and white line drawings illustrate the text. And to guide the reader looking for a particular quotation, three indices (two of which are annotated) are included: topical, author, and works of classical authors cited.

Best yet: a companion CD-Rom (0-86516-502-5) in the acclaimed Transparent Language Software is available...information can be found at the back of the book.

1
Līs lītem parit.
One lawsuit creates another.
(Anonymous)

2
Spem successus alit.
Success feeds hope.
(Anonymous)

3
Diēs dolōrem minuit.
Time diminishes grief.
*(Robert Burton, 1577–1640, English writer
and author of* The Anatomy of Melancholy)

4
Necessitās nōn habet lēgem.
Necessity does not know any law.
*(Bernard of Clairvaux, 1090–1153, French reformer of monastic life;
Oliver Cromwell in speech to Parliament 12 September 1654)*

5
Cucullus nōn facit monachum.
The cowl does not make the monk.
(Medieval)

6

Fidēs facit fidem.

Trust creates more trust.

(Anonymous)

7

Dītat Deus.

God enriches.

(Motto of Arizona)

8

Prīncipātus virum ostendit.

Leadership proves the man.

(Aristotle)

9

Vēritās.

Truth.

(Motto of Harvard University)

10

Stilus virum arguit.

The pencil (or style) reveals the man.

(Anonymous)

11

Senātus Populusque Rōmānus.
The Senate and the Roman People.

12

Injūria solvit amōrem.
Injury destroys love.
(Lucian)

13

Amat victōria cūram.
Victory likes careful preparation.
(Anonymus)

14

Facit indīgnātiō versum.
Indignation creates poetry.
(Juvenal, Satires 1.79)

15

Innocentia sēcūritātem affert.
Innocence brings security.
(Q. Curtius Rufus, 6.10.14, *adapted)*

16

Experientia docet.
Experience teaches.
(*Tacitus*, Histories 5.6)

17

Philosophum nōn facit barba.
A beard does not make a philosopher.
(*Plutarch, Greek philosopher and biographer, first–second centuries AD*)

18

Occāsiō facit fūrem.
Opportunity makes a thief.
(*Medieval*)

19

Gutta cavat lapidem.
A drop hollows out the stone.
(*Ovid*, Epistulae Ex Ponto 4.10.5)

20

Fugit hōra.
The hour is fleeing.
(*Persius*, 5.153)

21

Impedit īra animum.
Anger hinders the mind.
(*Dionysius Cato*, 2.4)

22

Asinus asinum fricat.
One donkey rubs another.
(*Anonymous*)

23

Nūdum latrō trānsmittit.
The robber passes by the person who does not have much.
(*Seneca*, Epistulae Morales 2.14.9)

24

Rēgnat populus.
The people rule.
(*Motto of Arkansas*)

25

Rēs pūblica virum docet.

Public affairs (or the State) teach a man.

(Plutarch, Greek biographer and philosopher, first–second centuries AD)

26

Sors aspera mōnstrat amīcum.

Bitter fortune shows a friend.

(Medieval)

27

Tōtam hodiē Circus Rōmam capit.

Today the Circus holds all of Rome.

(Juvenal, Satires 11.197)

28

Semper fidēlis.

Always faithful.

(Motto of U.S. Marine Corps)

29

Vincit vēritās.

Truth conquers.

(Motto)

30

Volēns et potēns.
Willing and able.
(Motto)

31

Brevitās dēlectat.
Brevity pleases.
(Medieval)

32

Patiēns et fortis sē ipsum fēlīcem facit.
The patient and brave man makes himself happy.
(Publilius Syrus, Sententia 464)

33

Sermō mollis frangit īram.
Soft speech dispels anger.
(Medieval)

34

Immodica īra gignit īnsāniam.
Uncontrolled anger creates insanity.
(Seneca, Epistulae Morales 2.18.14)

35

Sōla fidēs sufficit.
Faith alone is sufficient.
(Anonymous)

36

Umbram suam metuit.
He fears his own shadow.
(Quintus Tullius Cicero)

37

Quaelibet vulpēs caudam suam laudat.
Every fox praises his own tail.
(Anonymous)

38

Flōs ūnus nōn facit hortum.
One flower does not make a garden.
(Medieval)

39

Nōbilitat stultum vestis honesta virum.
Good clothes make even a stupid man appear noble.
(Medieval)

40

Sapientem locuplētat ipsa Nātūra.

Nature herself makes the wise man rich.
(Anonymous)

41

Rīvālitātem nōn amat victōria.

Victory does not like rivalry.
(Publilius Syrus, Sententia 575)

42

Sōla pecūnia rēgnat.

Money alone rules.
(Petronius, Satyricon 14)

43

Semper avārus eget.

The miser is always in need.
(Horace, Epistulae 1.2.56)

44

Pauperiem grandem vincit patientia tandem.

Patience finally conquers great poverty.
(Medieval)

45

Minuit praesentia fāmam.

Presence diminishes fame.

(Claudius Claudianus, Roman poet, fourth–fifth centuries AD)

46

Sua quemque fraus, suus timor maximē vexat.

His own deceit and his own fear trouble each person the most.

(Anonymous)

47

Una diēs aperit, cōnficit ūna diēs.

One day begins something, one day finishes it.

(Pseudo-Ausonius, 2.40)

48

Reus innocēns fortūnam, nōn testem, timet.

The innocent defendant fears fortune and not the witness.

(Publilius Syrus, Sententia 571)

49

Homō locum ōrnat, nōn hominem locus.

The man adorns his position, and the position does not adorn the man.

(Medieval)

50

Vānēscit absēns et novus intrat amor.
The absent love vanishes and the new love enters.
(*Ovid*, Ars Amatoria 2.358)

51

Lupus pilum mūtat, nōn mentem.
The wolf changes his hair (skin) but not his mind.
(*Anonymous*)

52

Ibī semper est victōria ubī concordia est.
Where there is concord there is always victory.
(*Publilius Syrus*, Sententia 289)

53

Mala dīgestiō, nūlla fēlicitās.
Bad digestion, no happiness.
(*Anonymous*)

54

Littera occīdit, spīritus autem vīvificat.
The letter kills but the spirit gives life.
(*Paul*, 2 Corinthians 3:6, *adapted [St. Jerome's Vulgate translation]*)

55

Fortiter, fidēliter, fēlīciter.
Bravely, faithfully, fortunately.
(Motto)

56

Quis...bene cēlat amōrem?
Who can successfully conceal love?
(Ovid, Heroides 12.39)

57

Deus vult.
God wills it.
(Battle cry of First Crusade)

58

Ut pānis ventrem, sīc pāscit lēctiō mentem.
As bread feeds the stomach, so reading fills the mind.
(Medieval)

59

Timidus vocat sē cautum, avārus parcum.
The timid person calls himself cautious, the miser calls himself thrifty.
(Anonymous)

60

Rēx rēgnat sed nōn gubernat.

The king rules but does not govern.

(Legal)

61

Honōs honestum decōrat, inhonestum notat.

An honor becomes an honorable person,
but it brands one who is not honorable.

(*Publilius Syrus,* Sententia 226)

62

**Jam frāter frātrem, jam fallit fīlia mātrem,
jamque pater nātum, jam fallit amīcus amīcum.**

Now brother deceives brother, daughter deceives mother,
father deceives son, and friend deceives friend.

(Medieval)

63

Homō prōpōnit sed Deus dispōnit.

Man proposes but God disposes.

(*Thomas à Kempis, German writer, 1380–1471,* De Imitatione Christi 1.19.2)

64
Sūs Minervam.
The pig is teaching Minerva.
(*M. Tullius Cicero*, Ad Familiares 9.18)

65
Ubī lībertās, ibī patria.
Where liberty is, there is my country.
(*Anonymous*)

66
Ex auriculā asinum.
One can recognize a donkey from his ear.
(*Anonymous*)

67
Latet anguis in herbā.
The snake is hiding in the grass.
(*Vergil*, Eclogues 3.93)

68

Palma nōn sine pulvere.
The palm not without dust.
(Motto)

69

Dē sōle caecus jūdicat.
The blind man is judging about the sun.
(Anonymous)

70

Prūdēns cum cūrā vivit, stultus sine cūrā.
The prudent man lives carefully, the stupid man carelessly.
(Medieval)

71

Victōria concordiā crēscit.
Victory increases with harmony.
(Motto)

72

Nēmō in amōre videt.
No one sees when he is in love.
(Propertius, 2.14.18)

73
Spēs mea in Deō.
My hope is in God.
(Motto)

74
Virtūte et operā.
With virtue and work.
(Motto)

75
Concordiā, integritāte, industriā.
With harmony, integrity, and industry.
(Motto)

76
Cōnstantiā et virtūte.
With constancy and virtue.
(Motto)

77
Numquam ex malō patre bonus fīlius.
There is never a good son from a bad father.
(Anonymous)

78
Nūlla rēgula sine exceptiōne.
No rule without an exception.
(Medieval)

79
Ex concordiā fēlīcitās.
Prosperity from harmony.
(Motto)

80
Nūlla diēs sine līneā.
No day without a line.
(Anonymous)

81
In sōlō Deō salūs.
Salvation lies in God alone.
(Motto)

82
Nēmō nisī suā culpā diū dolet.
No one grieves for a long time except through his own fault.
(Anonymous)

83

Flōs in pictūrā nōn est, nisī sōla figūra.

The flower in the picture does not exist, except just as a picture.

(Medieval)

84

Ut fragilis glaciēs, interit īra morā.

Just as fragile ice disappears, so anger disappears through delay.

(Ovid, Ars Amatoria 1.374)

85

In Venere semper dulcis est dēmentia.

In love there is always sweet madness.

(Publilius Syrus, Sententia 268)

86

Fidē et fortitūdine.

With faith and courage.

(Motto)

87

Vī et virtūte.

With force and with courage.

(Motto)

88

Scientia vēra cum fidē pūrā.
True knowledge with pure faith.
(Motto of Beloit College)

89

Sub pulchrā speciē latitat dēceptiō saepe.
Deception often lurks under a fair appearance.
(Medieval)

90

Ex ungue leōnem.
From the claw we can recognize the lion.
(Anonymous)

unguis

91

Nec spē nec metū.
Neither with hope nor with fear.
(Motto)

92

Fraus sublīmī rēgnat in aulā.
Deceit reigns in the lofty palace.
(*Seneca*, Phaedra 982)

93

Ubī amor, ibī oculus.
Where love is, there one's eye is.
(*Robert Burton, 1577–1640, English writer
and author of* The Anatomy of Melancholy)

94

Virtūte fidēque.
With courage and faith.
(*Motto*)

95

Nōn ūnō ictū arbor cadit.
A tree does not fall with (as a result of) one blow.
(*Medieval*)

96

Ubī bene, ibī patria.
Where things are prosperous, there is my homeland.
(*Anonymous*)

97

Inter dominum et servum nūlla amīcitia est.

Between master and slave there is no friendship.
(Q. Curtius Rufus, 7.8.28)

98

Saepe potēns jūstum premit ut rapidus lupus agnum.

Often the powerful man oppresses
the just man as the ravening wolf oppresses the lamb.
(Anonymous)

99

Claudus eget baculō, caecus duce, pauper amīcō.

The lame man needs a cane,
the blind man a guide, and the poor man a friend.
(Medieval)

lapis

pānis

100

Alterā manū fert lapidem, pānem ostentat alterā.

In one hand he holds a rock,
in the other hand
he is offering bread.
(Plautus, Aulularia 195)

101
Ignis nōn extinguitur igne.
Fire is not extinguished by fire.
(Medieval)

102
Amor tussisque nōn cēlātur.
Love and a cough are not concealed.
(Anonymous)

103
Trūditur diēs diē.
One day is pushed hard by another day.
(Horace, Odes 2.18.15)

104
Nūtrītur ventō, ventō restinguitur ignis.
Fire is nourished by wind, and it is also extinguished by wind.
(Ovid, Remedia Amoris 807)

105
Multitūdō nōn ratiōne dūcitur sed impetū.
The crowd is not led by reason but by impulse.
(Anonymous)

106
Amīcus in necessitāte probātur.
A friend is proven in time of necessity.
(Medieval)

107
Crux stat dum volvitur orbis.
The cross stands while the world turns.
(Motto of Carthusian monks, a Roman Catholic order,
founded in the 11th century at Chartreuse, France by St. Bruno)

108
Una quaeque arbor ex frūctū suō cognōscitur.
Each and every tree is known from its own fruit.
(Matthew 12.33, *adapted [St. Jerome's Vulgate translation]*)

109
Amphora sub veste numquam portātur honestē.
A jug is never carried under one's coat for any honorable reason.
(Medieval)

110
Nēmō laeditur nisī ā sē ipsō.
No one is harmed except by himself.
(Anonymous)

111

Sapiēns ut sōl permanet;
stultus autem ut lūna mūtātur.

The wise man remains as the sun; the foolish man changes as the moon.

(Medieval)

112

Antīquā veste pauper vestītur honestē.

The poor man is honorably clad in old clothes.

(Medieval)

113

Post jactūram quis nōn sapit?

Who is not wise after he has lost something?

(Anonymous)

114

Dē fūmō ad flammam.

From smoke to the fire.

(Ammianus Marcellinus, Roman historian, fourth century AD, 14.12)

115

Tūtus in mēnsā capitur angustā cibus.

Food is safely eaten at a narrow table.

(Seneca, Thyestes 452)

116

Virtūs, vel in hoste, laudātur.

Even in an enemy courage is praised.

(Anonymous)

117

Vulpēs nōn iterum capitur laqueō.

A fox is not caught a second time in a noose.

(Anonymous)

laqueus

118

Homō plantat, homō irrigat,
sed Deus dat incrēmentum.

Man plants, man waters, but God gives the increase.

(Motto of Merchant Taylor's School)

119

Pāx paritur bellō.

Peace is created by war.

(*Cornelius Nepos*, Epaminondas 5.4)

120

**Dē parvā scintillā magnum saepe
excitātur incendium.**

A great fire is often started from a small spark.

(*Anonymous*)

121

Saepe malum petitur, saepe bonum fugitur.

Evil is often sought, and good is often fled from.

(*Anonymous*)

122

In vīnō, in irā, in puerō semper est vēritās.

Truth always exists in wine, in anger, and in a child.

(*Anonymous*)

123

Vīnō forma perit, vīnō corrumpitur aetās.

Beauty perishes by wine (and) by wine youth is destroyed.

(*Anonymous*)

124

Ira odium generat, concordia nūtrit amōrem.

Anger creates hatred, harmony nourishes love.

(*Dionysius Cato*, 1.36)

125

Ex vitiō sapiēns aliēnō ēmendat suum.

The wise man corrects his own fault from the fault of someone else.

(*Publilius Syrus*, Sententia 150)

126

Dum fēlēs dormit, mūs gaudet et exsilit antrō.

While a cat sleeps, the mouse rejoices and leaps from his hole.

(*Medieval*)

127

Mulier rēctē olet ubī nihil olet.

A woman smells right when she does not smell at all.

(*Plautus*, Mostellaria 273)

128

Prō bonō pūblicō.

For the public good.

(Commonplace)

129

Saepe est etiam sub palliolō sordidō sapientia.

There is often wisdom under a dirty cloak.

(Caecilius Statius, 255 [cited by Cicero, Tusculanae Disputationes 3.23, 56])

130

Crēscit audācia experīmentō.

Boldness increases through trial.

(Pliny the Younger, Epistulae 9.33.6)

131

Rārō senex mūtat sententiam.

An old man rarely changes his mind.

(Medieval)

132

Studium generat studium, īgnāvia īgnāviam.

Enthusiasm creates enthusiasm, while laziness creates more laziness.

(Anonymous)

133

Sōla virtūs praestat gaudium perpetuum, sēcūrum.

Only virtue furnishes joy that is perpetual and secure.

(*Seneca*, Epistulae Morales 3.27.3)

134

Conjugium sine prōle, diēs velutī sine sōle.

Marriage without offspring is like the day without the sun.

(*Anonymous*)

135

**Tūtus in mēnsā capitur angustā cibus;
venēnum in aurō bibitur.**

Food is eaten in safety at a narrow table,
but poison is drunk out of golden cups.

(*Seneca*, Thyestes 452–53)

136

Ferrum ferrō exacuitur.

Iron is sharpened by iron.

(Proverbs 27.17 [*St. Jerome's Vulgate translation*])

137

Nōn lupus ad studium sed mentem vertit ad agnum.
The wolf turns his attention not toward his studies but toward the lamb.
(Medieval)

138

Dē sapientī virō facit īra virum citō stultum.
Anger quickly makes a stupid man out of a wise one.
(Medieval)

139

Virtūte et meritō.
With courage and merit.
(Motto)

140

Tempus fugit.
Time flies.
(Commonplace)

141

Prōpositum mūtat sapiēns, at stultus inhaeret.
A wise man changes his proposal, but a stupid man clings to it.
(Petrarch)

142
Gladiātor in arēnā cōnsilium capit.
The gladiator makes up his mind in the arena.
(*Seneca*, Epistulae Morales 3.22.1, *adapted*)

143
Lēx pūnit mendācium.
The law punishes lying.
(*Legal*)

144
Nātūra abhorret vacuum.
Nature abhors a vacuum.
(*Baruch Spinoza, 1632–1677, Dutch philosopher*; Ethics, Part 1 Proposition 15 [note])

145
Omnis in ferrō est salūs.
Every safety lies in steel.
(*Seneca*, Hercules Furens 342)

146
Vēritās odium parit.
Truth creates hatred.
(*Robert Burton, 1577–1640, English writer
and author of* The Anatomy of Melancholy)

147
Exitus in dubiō est.
The result is in doubt.
(*Ovid*, Metamorphoses 12.522)

148
Caelum ipsum petitur stultitiā.
Heaven itself is sought through foolishness.
(*Robert Burton, 1577–1640, English writer*
and author of The Anatomy of Melancholy)

149
Ex aliēnō perīculō sapiēns sē corrigit et ēmendat.
From the example of someone else's difficulties,
the wise man changes and corrects himself.
(*Medieval*)

150
Mala herba citō crēscit.
A weed grows quickly.
(*Anonymous*)

151
Comes fācundus in viā prō vehiculō est.
On a journey a witty companion is as good as a ride.
(*Publilius Syrus*, Sententia 104)

152

Nēmō nisī vitiō suō miser est.

No one is unhappy except through his own fault.

(*Seneca,* Epistulae Morales 8.70.15)

153

Tua rēs agitur, pariēs cum proximus ardet.

Your affairs are at stake when the wall nearest to you is on fire.

(*Horace,* Epistulae 1.18.84)

154

Commūne perīculum concordiam parit.

Common danger creates concord.

(*Anonymous*)

155

Prīma dīgestiō fit in ōre.

The first digestion takes place in the mouth.

(*Anonymous*)

156

Malum vās nōn frangitur.

The bad vase does not get broken.

(*Anonymous*)

157

Perenne conjugium animus, nōn corpus, facit.

Personality and not physical beauty makes a marriage lasting.

(Publilius Syrus, Sententia 481)

158

Homō semper aliud, Fortūna aliud cōgitat.

Man always plans one thing, and Fortune plans something else.

(Publilius Syrus, Sententia 216, adapted)

159

Obit anus, abit onus.

The old lady is dead, the burden has passed on.

(Schopenhauer, 1788–1860)

160

Ut vēr dat flōrem, studium sīc reddit honōrem.

As spring brings flowers, so study brings honors.

(Medieval)

161

Una hirundō nōn facit vēr.

One swallow does not make a spring.

(Anonymous)

162

In caudā venēnum.
There is poison in the tail.
(*Anonymous*)

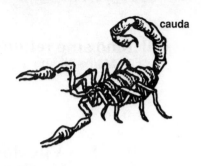

cauda

163

In marī aquam quaerit.
He is looking for water in the ocean.
(*Medieval*)

164

Terminat hōra diem; terminat auctor opus.
The hour finishes the day; the author finishes his work.
(*Christopher Marlowe, 1564–1593*)

165

Ovem in fronte, vulpem in corde gerit.
He acts like a sheep in his face but like a fox in his heart.
(*Medieval*)

166

Nūllum sine exitū iter est.
There is no journey without an end.
(*Seneca*, Epistulae Morales 8.77.13)

167

Homō sine religiōne sīc ut equus sine frēnō.

Man without religion is like a horse without a bridle.

(Medieval)

168

Vīle dōnum, vīlis grātia.

Cheap gift, cheap thanks.

(Anonymous)

169

Est vērum verbum: frangit Deus omne superbum.

It is a true word: God breaks everything which is haughty.

(Medieval)

170

Numquam aliud nātūra, aliud sapientia dīcit.

Nature never says one thing and wisdom something else.

(Juvenal, Satires 14.321)

171

Malum nūllum est sine aliquō bonō.

There is no evil without some good.

(Pliny the Elder)

172

Mōbile mūtātur semper cum prīncipe vulgus.

The fickle crowd always changes with its leader.
(Medieval)

173

Omne īgnōtum prō magnificō est.

Everything unknown is considered to be magnificent.
(*Tacitus*, Agricola 30)

174

Nīl bene pauper agit.

A poor man does nothing well.
(Medieval)

175

Aliēnō in locō haud stabile rēgnum est.

There is no stable rule in someone else's position.
(*Seneca*, Hercules Furens 344)

176

Ubī est thēsaurus tuus, ibī est et cor tuum.

Where your treasure is, there is your heart also.
(Matthew 6.21 *[St. Jerome's Vulgate translation]*)

177
Nihil rēctē sine exemplō docētur aut discitur.
Nothing is rightly taught or learned without examples.
(*Columella*, 11.1.4)

178
Suāviter et fortiter.
Kindly and courageously.
(*Motto*)

179
Interdum stabulum reparātur post grave damnum.
Sometimes the stable is repaired after serious loss.
(*Medieval*)

180
Simile similī gaudet.
Like rejoices in like.
(*Medieval*)

181
Virtūte et nūmine.
With courage and with divinity.
(*Motto*)

182
Ab honestō virum bonum nihil dēterret.
Nothing deters a good man from what is honorable.
(*Seneca*, Epistulae Morales 7.6.18)

183
Virēscit vulnere virtūs.
Virtue grows powerful by wounds.
(*Motto*)

184
Aut Caesar aut nihil.
Either Caesar or nothing.
(*Motto of Cesare Borgia, 1476–1507, Italian cardinal, political and military leader, and son of Pope Alexander VI, Rodrigo Borgia*)

185
Quam miserum est ubī cōnsilium cāsū vincitur!
How unfortunate it is when planning is upset by chance!
(*Publilius Syrus*, Sententia 549)

186
Crīmine nēmō caret.
No one is free from accusation of wrong doing.
(*Anonymous*)

187

Bēstia quaeque suōs nātōs cum laude corōnat.

Every animal crowns its own children with praise.

(Medieval)

188

Obsequium amīcōs, vēritās odium parit.

Compliance makes friends, the truth creates hatred.

(Terence, Andria 68)

189

Tranquillās etiam naufragus horret aquās.

The shipwrecked man is afraid even of quiet waters.

(Ovid, Epistulae Ex Ponto 2.7.8)

190

Faciēs tua computat annōs.

Your face shows (counts) your years.

(Juvenal, Satires 6.199)

191

Fēlīcitās multōs habet amīcōs.

Prosperity has many friends.

(Erasmus, 1466–1536, Dutch humanist, theologian, and scholar)

192
In oculīs animus habitat.
Our personality lives in our eyes.
(Pliny the Younger, Epistulae 9.36.2, *adapted)*

193
Homicidium, cum admittunt singulī, crīmen est; virtūs vocātur cum pūblicē geritur.
When individuals commit it, murder is a crime;
it is called a virtue when it is done publicly.
(Cyprian, died AD 258)

194
Paucī sed bonī.
Few men, but good ones.
(Commonplace)

195
Tempore fēlīcī multī numerantur amīcī.
In prosperous times many friends are counted.
(Medieval)

196
Post tenebrās lūx.
After the darkness comes light.
(Anonymous)

197
Quaerit aquās in aquīs.
He is looking for water in the middle of water.
(*Ovid*, Amores 2.2.43)

198
Fidē et litterīs.
With faith and education.
(*Motto of St. Paul's School, London*)

199
Litterae nōn dant pānem.
Literature does not earn bread.
(*Medieval*)

200
Multī morbī cūrantur abstinentiā.
Many diseases are cured by abstinence.
(*Celsus*, 1.2.8, *adapted*)

201
Cum sēsē vincit sapiēns, minimē vincitur.
When a wise man conquers himself, he is conquered least of all.
(*Publilius Syrus*, Sententia 654)

202

Oculī amōrem incipiunt, cōnsuētūdō perficit.

Eyes begin a love affair, association brings it to fulfillment.

(Publilius Syrus)

203

Malī corvī, malum ōvum.

Bad crows, bad egg.

(Anonymous)

204

Superbus et avārus numquam quiēscunt.

The haughty person and the miser never are at rest.

(Anonymous)

205

Mortuī nōn dolent.

The dead do not grieve.

(Medieval)

206

Certō veniunt ōrdine Parcae.

The Fates come in fixed order.
(*Seneca*, Hercules Furens 188)

207

Pars major lacrimās rīdet et intus habet.

The majority laughs at tears but has them within themselves.
(*Martial*, 10.80.6)

208

Famēs commendat cibōs: nihil contemnit ēsuriēns.

Hunger recommends food; the hungry man despises nothing.
(*Anonymous*)

209

Dīvitiae apud sapientem virum in servitūte sunt, apud stultum in imperiō.

With a wise man riches are in servitude; with a stupid man,
they are in control.
(*Seneca*, De Vita Beata 26.1)

210

Nōscitur ex sociīs.

He is known from his companions.
(*Anonymous*)

211
Fabās indulcat famēs.
Hunger makes (even) beans pleasant.
(Anonymous)

212
Prīnceps injūstus servōs habet et vitiōsōs.
An unjust ruler also has bad slaves.
(Medieval)

213
Dīvitiae pariunt cūrās.
Riches bring cares.
(Medieval)

214
Generōsōs animōs labor nūtrit.
Hard work nourishes noble minds.
(Seneca, Epistulae Morales 4.31.5)

215
Dēcipit frōns prīma multōs.
The first appearance deceives many people.
(Phaedrus, 4.2.5–6)

216

Dē mortuīs nīl nisī bonum.

About the dead nothing except good.

(Diogenes Laertius, fl. AD 200)

217

Miseram servitūtem falsō pācem vocant.

They falsely call miserable slavery peace.

(Tacitus, Histories 4.17)

218

Elephās Indus culicēs nōn timet.

The Indian elephant does not fear gnats.

(Anonymous)

219

Nātūra in operātiōnibus suīs nōn facit saltum.

In its activities nature does not make a sudden leap.

(Carl von Linné, Swedish botanist, 1707–1778, Philosophia Botanica *Section 77)*

220

Per undās et ignēs fluctuat nec mergitur.

It floats through waves and fire and does not sink.

(Motto of Paris)

221
Multīs ictibus dējicitur quercus.
The oak is thrown down by many blows.
(*Anonymous*)

222
Dominus vōbīscum et cum spīritū tuō.
God be with you and with thy spirit.
(*Ecclesiastical*)

223
Laus alit artēs.
Praise nourishes the arts.
(*Seneca*, Epistulae Morales 102.16.7)

224
Necessitūdō...etiam timidōs fortēs facit.
Necessity makes even timid people brave.
(*Sallust*, Catiline 58.19)

225
Audācēs Fortūna juvat timidōsque repellit.
Fortune aids the bold and repels the timid.
(*Anonymous*)

226
Ubī mel, ibī apēs.
Where there is honey, there are bees.
(Anonymous)

227
Fontibus ex modicīs concrēscit maximus amnis.
The greatest stream increases from small springs.
(Medieval)

228
Bonus pāstor animam suam dat prō ovibus suīs.
The good shepherd gives his life for his sheep.
(John 10.11 *[St. Jerome's Vulgate translation]*)

229
Crēscunt sermōnēs ubī conveniunt mulierēs.
Talk increases where women gather.

(Medieval)

230

Hominēs, dum docent, discunt.
While men teach, they learn.
(*Seneca*, Epistulae Morales 1.7.8)

231

**Urbēs cōnstituit aetās, hōra dissolvit.
Momentō fit cinis, diū silva.**
A period of time builds up cities, a single hour destroys them.
In a moment something becomes a cinder which for a long time was a wood.
(*Seneca*, Naturales Quaestiones 3.27.2)

232

Sēra...tacitīs poena venit pedibus.
Punishment comes late on silent feet.
(*Tibullus*, 1.9.4)

233

Ignis aurum probat, miseria fortēs virōs.
Fire tests gold, misfortune tests brave men.
(*Anonymous*)

234

In magnō magnī capiuntur flūmine piscēs.
Large fish are captured in large rivers.
(*Anonymous*)

235

Modus omnibus in rēbus.

Moderation in all things.

(*Plautus*, Poenulus 238)

236

Vulpēs pilum mūtat, nōn mōrēs.

The fox changes his skin but not his habits.

(*Suetonius*, Vespasian 16.3)

237

Interdum audācēs efficit ipse timor.

Sometimes fear itself makes people brave.

(*Medieval*)

238

Nōn bene sub stabulō nūtriuntur ovēs aliēnō.

Sheep are not well taken care of in somebody else's stable.

(*Medieval*)

239

Hōrae quidem cēdunt et diēs et mēnsēs et annī, nec praeteritum tempus umquam revertitur.

The hours pass and the days and the months and the years, and the past time never returns.

(*M. Tullius Cicero*, De Senectute 69)

240

Amīcitia parēs aut accipit aut facit.

Friendship either accepts equals or makes them equals.
(Translation of Aristotle)

241

Sunt quidem hominēs nōn rē sed nōmine.

They are men not in fact but only in name.
(Anonymous)

242

Aequat omnēs cinis.

Death makes everyone equal.
(*Seneca,* Epistulae Morales 14.91.16)

243

**Multae sunt arborēs, sed nōn omnēs faciunt frūctum;
multī frūctūs, sed nōn omnēs comēstibilēs.**

There are many trees, but not all of them bear fruit;
there are many fruits, but not all of them are edible.
(*Petrus Alphonsus,* Disciplina Clericalis 22 [De libris non credendis] p. 31)

244

Mōribus antīquīs rēs stat Rōmāna virīsque.

The Roman state stands because of its ancient customs and men.
(Ennius, incerta)

245

Labōrēs pariunt honōrēs.
Hard work brings about honors.
(*Medieval*)

246

**Caecī vident, claudī ambulant,
leprōsī mundantur, surdī audiunt, mortuī resurgunt,
pauperēs ēvangelizantur.**
The blind see, the lame walk,
the lepers are healed, the deaf hear, the dead rise,
and the poor have the gospel preached unto them.
(Matthew 11.5 [*St. Jerome's Vulgate translation*])

247

Lēgēs...bonae ex malīs mōribus prōcreantur.
Good laws arise from evil customs.
(*Macrobius*, Saturnalia 3.17.10)

248

Omnēs ūna manet nox.
One night remains for us all.
(*Horace*, Odes 1.28.15)

249
Concordiā parvae rēs crēscunt.
Even modest affairs (farms, fortunes, etc.) prosper with harmony.
(*Sallust*, Jugurtha 10.11)

250
Post cinerēs est vērus honor, est glōria vēra.
After death comes true honor and true glory.
(*Medieval*)

251
Jūs superat vīrēs.
Right overcomes might.
(*Anonymous*)

252
Abūsus nōn tollit ūsūs.
Abuse does not take away the right to use.
(*Legal*)

253
In pāce leōnēs, in proeliō cervī.
They are lions in times of peace and deer in battle.
(*Tertullian*)

254
Artēs, scientia, vēritās.
Arts, science, truth.
(Motto of The University of Michigan)

255
Aurum flamma probat, hominēs temptātiō justōs.
Flame tests gold, temptation tests just men.
(Anonymous)

256
Aufert os canibus canis ūnus saepe duōbus.
Often one dog takes a bone away from two dogs.
(Medieval)

257
Tūtī sunt omnēs, ūnus ubī dēfenditur.
All are safe where one person is defended.
(Publilius Syrus, Sententia 686)

258
Unguibus et rōstrō.
With claws and beak.
(Anonymous)

259
Lēge dūrā vīvunt mulierēs.
Women live under a harsh law.
(*Plautus*, Mercator 817)

260
Bonōs corrumpunt mōrēs congressūs malī.
Evil communications corrupt good manners.
(*Tertullian*)

261
Ubī opēs, ibī amīcī.
Where wealth is, there friends are.
(*Anonymous*)

262
Lātrantem cūratne alta Diāna canem?
Does Diana on high care about the barking dog?
(*Anonymous*)

Diāna

263

Impia sub dulcī melle venēna jacent.

Wicked poisons lie under sweet honey.

(*Ovid*, Amores 1.8.104)

264

Multōs morbōs multa fercula ferunt.

Many courses bring many diseases.

(*Pliny the Elder*)

265

Vulgus ex vēritāte pauca, ex opīniōne multa aestimat.

The people judge a few things by their truth, and many by their opinion.

(*M. Tullius Cicero*, Pro Roscio Comoedeo 29)

266

Labor omnia vincit.

Labor conquers all things.

(*Vergil*, Georgics 1.145)

267

Juppiter in caelīs, Caesar regit omnia terrīs.

Jupiter rules everything in the sky, Caesar rules everything on earth.

(*Anonymous*)

268

Dē minimīs nōn cūrat lēx.

The law does not care about trifles.

(Legal)

269

Vulpēs nōn capitur mūneribus.

A fox is not caught by gifts.

(Medieval)

270

Dum vītant stultī vitia, in contrāria currunt.

When stupid people avoid faults, they run into the opposite faults.

(Horace, Satires 1.2.24)

271

Astra regunt hominēs, sed regit astra Deus.

The stars rule men, but God rules the stars.

(Anonymous)

272

Nōn redit unda fluēns; nōn redit hōra ruēns.

A flowing wave does not return; the rushing hour does not return.

(Medieval)

273

Stultus verbīs nōn corrigitur.

The stupid man is not corrected by words.

(Medieval)

274

Carmina nōn dant pānem.

Poetry does not bring bread.

(Anonymous)

275

Silent...lēgēs inter arma.

In time of war the laws are silent.

(M. Tullius Cicero, Pro Milone 4.10)

276

Multa senem circumveniunt incommoda.

Many inconveniences surround an old man.

(Anonymous)

277

Pauca sed bona.

Few things but good ones.

(Anonymous)

278
Ratiō omnia vincit.
Reason conquers all things.
(Anonymous)

279
Variat omnia tempus.
Time changes everything.
(Anonymous)

280
Verba movent, exempla trahunt.
Words move people, examples draw them on.
(Anonymous)

281
Facta, nōn verba.
Deeds, not words.
(Commonplace)

282
Ācta exteriōra indicant interiōra sēcrēta.
Exterior acts indicate interior secrets.
(Legal)

283
Virtūte, nōn verbīs.
With courage, not words.
(Motto)

284
Ignis, mare, mulier: tria mala.
Fire, sea, woman: three bad things.
(Medieval)

285
Furor arma ministrat.
Anger furnishes arms.
(Vergil, Aeneid 1.150)

286
Fīdus in adversīs cognōscitur omnis amīcus.
A faithful friend is recognized in adverse circumstances.
(Anonymous)

287
Studiīs et rēbus honestīs.
Through study and honest activities.
(Motto)

288

Virtūte et armīs.

With courage and arms.
(Motto of Mississippi)

289

Venter praecepta nōn audit.

The stomach does not hear advice.
(Seneca, Epistulae Morales 2.21.11)

290

Acta deōs numquam mortālia fallunt.

Mortal acts never fool the gods.
(Ovid, Tristia 1.2.95)

291

Deō adjuvante.

With God helping.
(Motto)

292

Duōbus lītigantibus, tertius gaudet.

When two people are quarreling, the third gets the profit.
(Medieval)

293
Deō volente.
With God willing.
(Commonplace)

294
Saevīs pāx quaeritur armīs.
Peace is sought by savage arms.
(Statius, Thebaid 4.554)

295
Ostendit sermō mōrēs animumque latentem.
A person's speech shows his character and his inner personality.
(Medieval)

296
Saepe summa ingenia in occultō latent.
Often the greatest minds lie hidden.
(Plautus, Captivi 165)

297
Lātrante ūnō, lātrat statim et alter canis.
When one dog barks, another dog immediately starts to bark.
(Anonymous)

298

Multa sub vultū odia, multa sub ōsculō latent.

Many types of hatred lie hidden
under a pleasant expression and (even) under a kiss.
(Medieval)

299

Saepe tacēns vōcem verbaque vultus habet.

Often a silent face has voice and words.
(Ovid, Ars Amatoria 1.574)

300

Deō dūcente.

With God leading.
(Commonplace)

301

Crēscit in adversis virtūs.

Courage increases in dangerous circumstances.
(Lucan, Pharsalia 3.614)

302

Saepe, premente deō, fert deus alter opem.

Often, when one god is hostile, another god brings help.
(Ovid, Tristia 1.2.4)

303
Similia similibus cūrantur.
Like things are cured by like.
(Samuel Hahnemann, 1755–1843, German physician)

304
Non omnis fert omnia tellūs.
Not every land brings forth all kinds of fruit.
(Anonymous)

305
Jējūnus venter nōn audit verba libenter.
A hungry stomach does not gladly listen to speeches.
(Medieval)

306
Aliquis in omnibus, nūllus in singulīs.
Somebody in all areas of endeavor, nobody in separate matters.
*(Robert Burton, 1577–1640, English writer
and author of* The Anatomy of Melancholy)

307
Verba dat omnis amor.
Every lover deceives the person he loves.
(Ovid, Remedia Amoris 95)

308

Multum, nōn multa.

Much, not many.

(*Pliny the Younger*, Epistulae 7.9.15)

309

Dē hōc multī multa, omnēs aliquid, nēmō satis.

Concerning this, many people know much, everybody knows something,
and nobody knows enough.

(*Anonymous*)

310

Piscis captīvus vīnum vult, flūmina vīvus.

A fish when caught needs wine, a live fish needs the river.

(*Medieval*)

311

Ipsa scientia potestās est.

Knowledge itself is power.

(*Sir Francis Bacon, 1561–1626, English philosopher and essayist*)

312

Plumbum aurum fit.

Lead becomes gold.

(*Petronius*, Satyricon 43, *adapted*)

313

Nēmō...patriam quia magna est amat, sed quia sua.

No one loves his country because it is big but because it is his own.
(*Seneca*, Epistlulae Morales 66.26)

314

Post calamitātem memoria alia est calamitās.

After a disaster, the memory of it is another disaster.
(*Publilius Syrus*, Sententia 497)

315

ōscula, nōn oculī, sunt in amōre ducēs.

Kisses, and not eyes, are the leaders in love.
(*Anonymous*)

316

Formōsa faciēs mūta commendātiō est.

A pretty face is a silent commendation.
(*Publilius Syrus*, Sententia 169)

317

Nōn est ad astra mollis ē terrīs via.

The trip from the earth to the stars is not an easy one.
(*Seneca*, Hercules Furens 437)

318
Famēs est optimus coquus.
Hunger is the best cook.
(Anonymous)

319
Nēmo malus fēlīx.
No bad man is happy.
(Juvenal, Satires 4.8)

320
Rēs est forma fugāx.
Beauty is a fleeting thing.
(Seneca, Phaedra 773)

321
Habet Deus suās hōrās et morās.
God has his hours and his delays.
(Anonymous)

322
Nōbilitās sōla est atque ūnica virtūs.
Virtue is the sole and only kind of nobility.
(Juvenal, Satires 8.20)

323

Senectūs ipsa est morbus.
Old age all by itself is a disease.
(*Terence*, Phormio 575)

324

Nīl sub sōle novum.
Nothing new under the sun.
(Ecclesiastes 1.10 [*St. Jerome's Vulgate translation*])

325

Fortūna caeca est.
Fortune is blind.
(*Anonymous*)

326

Rēbus in hūmānīs Rēgīna Pecūnia nauta est.
In human affairs Queen Money is the one who runs the ship.
(*Medieval*)

327

Amīcus vērus rāra avis.
A true friend is a rare bird.
(*Medieval*)

328

Fortūna numquam perpetuō est bona.
Fortune is never always good.
*(Robert Burton, 1577–1640, English writer
and author of* The Anatomy of Melancholy*)*

329

Montānī semper līberī.
Mountaineers are always free.
(Motto of West Virginia)

330

Patientia rāra virtūs.
Patience is a rare virtue.
(Anonymous)

331

Dominus illūminātiō mea.
God is my light.
(Motto of Oxford University)

332

Mors tua vīta mea.
Your death is my life.
(Anonymous)

333

Nūlla terra exilium est sed altera patria.
No land is an exile but simply another native land.
(*Seneca*, De Remediis Fortuitorum 8.1)

334

Vāna est sine vīribus īra.
Anger without strength to enforce it is empty.
(*Anonymous*)

335

Nūlla calamitās sōla.
Disaster is never alone. *It never rains but it pours.*
(*Anonymous*)

336

Vir bonus est animal rārum.
A good man is a rare creature.
(*Medieval*)

337

Est certum praesēns, sed sunt incerta futūra.
The present is certain, but the future is uncertain.
(*Medieval*)

338

Sōla nōbilitās virtūs.

Courage is the only real nobility.
(Motto)

339

Litterae sine mōribus vānae.

Education without good morals is useless.
(Motto of University of Pennsylvania)

340

Salūs pūblica suprēma lēx.

The public safety is the supreme law.
(Legal)

341

Longum iter est per praecepta,
breve et efficāx per exempla.

The journey is long through advice, but short and efficient through examples.
(Seneca, Epistlulae Morales 6.5)

342
Maximum mīrāculum homō sapiēns.
A wise man is the greatest of all miracles.
(Hermes Trismegistus, Thrice-Greatest Hermes,
supposed author of occult works based on Egyptian lore)

343
Optima medicīna temperantia est.
The best medicine is moderation.
(Anonymous)

344
Nōmen amīcitia est, nōmen ināne fidēs.
Friendship is just a name, trust is just an empty name.
(Ovid, Ars Amatoris 1.740)

345
Varium et mūtābile semper fēmina.
Woman is always a fickle and changeable thing.
(Vergil, Aeneid 4.569)
(Ironically, it is Aeneas the man who abandons Dido the woman)

346
Spīritus quidem prōmptus est, carō vērō īnfirma.
The spirit is willing but the flesh is weak.
(Mark 14.38 *[St. Jerome's Vulgate translation]*)

347

Victōria nātūrā est īnsolēns et superba.

By its nature victory is insolent and haughty.
(*M. Tullius Cicero*, Pro Marcello 3.9, *adapted*)

348

Dulce pōmum cum abest custōs.

The apple is sweet when the watchman is absent.
(*Anonymous*)

349

Necessitās...ultimum ac maximum tēlum est.

Necessity is the last and greatest weapon.
(*Livy*, Ab Urbe Condita 4.28, *adapted*)

350

Laudātur ab hīs, culpātur ab illīs.

He is praised by some, blamed by others.
(*Horace*, Satires 1.2.11)

351

Nūllīs amor est sānābilis herbīs.

Love is curable by no herbs.
(*Ovid*, Metamorphoses 1.523)

352

Malus bonum ubī sē simulat tunc est pessimus.

When a bad man pretends that he is a good man, then he is at his worst.
(*Publilius Syrus*, Sententia 317)

353

Post hoc, propter hoc.

After something, because of something.
(*Commonplace; A fallacy in logic*)

354

Crūdēlis est in rē adversā objūrgātiō.

When a person is in trouble, scolding him is a cruel thing to do.
(*Publilius Syrus*, Sententia 86)

355

Unus vir, nūllus vir.

One man, no man.
(*Medieval*)

356

Cum jocus est vērus, jocus est malus atque sevērus.

When a joke is true, the joke is a bad thing and a cruel thing.
(*Medieval*)

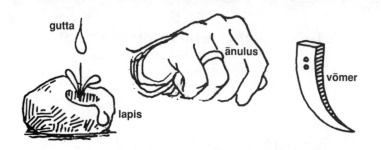

357

**Gutta cavat lapidem, cōnsūmitur ānulus ūsū,
et teritur pressā vōmer aduncus humō.**

Dropping water wears away a stone, a ring is worn out with use,
and the curved plowshare is ground down by the earth it presses.
(*Ovid*, Epistulae Ex Ponto 4.10.5–6)

358

Struit īnsidiās lacrīmīs cum fēmina plōrat.

When a woman weeps she is preparing an ambush with her tears.
(*Dionysius Cato*, 3.20)

359

Aspiciunt oculīs superī mortālia jūstīs.

The gods look on mortal acts with just eyes.
(*Ovid*, Metamorphoses 13.70)

360

In angustīs amīcī bonī appārent.

Good friends appear in difficulties.

(Anonymous)

361

Homō sōlitārius aut deus aut bēstia.

A man by himself is either a god or a beast.

(Aristotle, 384–322 BC, Politics 1.2)

362

Simul et dictum et factum.

At once said and done.

(Anonymous)

363

Otia corpus alunt; animus quoque pāscitur illīs.

Leisure nourishes the body; the mind also is fed by leisure.

(Ovid, Epistulae Ex Ponto 1.4.21)

364

Ōtium sine litterīs mors est.

Leisure without reading is death.

(Seneca, Epistlulae Morales 82.3)

365

Forma virōs neglēcta decet.

A careless appearance is suitable for men.

(*Ovid*, Ars Amatoria 1.509)

366

Dictum, factum.

Said, done.

(*Terence,* Andria 381, *adapted*)

367

Quī tenet anguillam per caudam nōn habet illam.

Who holds an eel by the tail does not (really) hold him.

(*Medieval*)

368

Nihil est...simul et inventum et perfectum.

Nothing is at once discovered and perfected.

(*M. Tullius Cicero*, Brutus 70)

369

Jūcundī āctī labōrēs.

Past labors are pleasant.

(*M. Tullius Cicero*, De finibus 2.32.105)

370

Concordia rēs est in rēbus maximē adversīs ūtilis.

In situations which are particularly unfavorable, harmony is a useful thing.
(*Anonymous*)

371

Saxum volūtum nōn obdūcitur muscō.

A rolling stone is not covered with moss. *A rolling stone gathers no moss.*
(*Anonymous*)

372

Semel ēmissum volat irreparābile verbum.

A word once spoken flies away and cannot be recovered.
(*Horace,* Epistulae 1.18.71)

373

Fūmum fugiēns in ignem incidit.

Fleeing smoke, he falls into the fire.
Out of the frying pan, into the fire.
(*Medieval*)

374

Ex pede Herculem.

From his foot we can recognize Hercules.
(*Anonymous*)

375

Vēr nōn ūna diēs, nōn ūna redūcit hirundō.

One day does not bring spring, nor does one swallow.
One swallow does not make a summer.
(*Anonymous*)

376

Fīnis corōnat opus.

The end crowns the work.
(*Medieval*)

377

Nūmen, lūmen.

God and light.
(*Motto of Wisconsin*)

378

Leōnem mortuum et catulī mordent.

Even puppies bite a dead lion.
(*Medieval*)

379

Multa docet famēs.

Hunger teaches us much.
(*Anonymous*)

380
Jējūnus rārō stomachus vulgāria temnit.
A hungry stomach rarely despises common food.
(*Horace*, Satires 2.2.38)

381
Deō juvante.
With God helping.
(*Motto*)

382
Vincit omnia vēritās.
Truth conquers all.
(*Motto*)

383
Magna cīvitās magna sōlitūdō.
A great city is a great solitude.
(*Anonymous*)

384
Amor magister est optimus.
Love is the best teacher.
(*Pliny the Younger*, Epistulae 4.19.4, *adapted*)

385

In fugā foeda mors est; in victōriā, glōriōsa.

In flight, death is disgraceful; in victory, it is glorious.

(*M. Tullius Cicero*, Philippics 14.12.32)

386

Aliud vīnum, aliud ēbrietās.

Wine is one thing, drunkenness is something else.

(*Anonymous*)

387

Nēmō suā sorte contentus.

No one is content with his lot.

(*Anonymous*)

388

Facile est imperium in bonīs.

Rule over good people is easy.

(*Plautus*, Miles Gloriosus 611)

389

Quis pauper? Avārus.

Who is the poor man? The miser.

(*Pseudo-Ausonius*, 1.1.3)

390

Omne initium est difficile.

Every beginning is difficult.

(Anonymous)

391

Omnibus in rēbus gravis est inceptiō prīma.

In all things the first undertaking is hard.

(Anonymous)

392

Nigrum in candida vertunt.

They turn black into white.

(Juvenal, Satires 3.30)

393

Duce tempus eget.

The times need a leader.

(Lucan, Pharsalia 7.88, adapted)

394

Nūlla diēs maerōre caret.

No day lacks sorrow.

(Medieval)

395
Dōtāta mulier virum regit.
A woman who comes with a dowry controls her husband.
(Anonymous)

396
Multī enim sunt vocātī, paucī vērō ēlēctī.
For many are called, but few are chosen.
(Matthew 20.16 *[St. Jerome's Vulgate translation]*)

397
Nōn sine causā sed sine fīne laudātus.
He is praised not without reason but without end.
(Anonymous)

398
Ubī peccat aetās major, male discit minor.
When the older generation makes mistakes,
the younger generation learns bad habits.
(*Publilius Syrus,* Sententia 633)

399
Omnis īnstabilis et incerta fēlīcitās est.
Every prosperity is unstable and uncertain.
(*Seneca the Elder,* Controversiae 1.1.3)

400
Virtūs mīlle scūta.
Courage is a thousand shields.
(Motto)

401
Mea anima est tamquam tabula rāsa.
My mind is like a clean tablet.
(Paul of Venice, ca. 1369–1429, theologian and philosopher [Aristotle's De Anima
430^a *attributed])*

402
Sua multī āmittunt, cupidē dum aliēna appetunt.
Many lose their own belongings
while they greedily seek belongings of others.
(Anonymous)

403
Jūs summum saepe summa est malitia.
The highest law is often the highest evil.
(Terence, Heauton Timoroumenos 796*)*

404
Nōn bene flat flammam quī continet ōre farīnam.
It is not a good idea
for a person who has flour in his mouth to blow a flame out.

(Medieval)

405
Fēlīciter sapit
quī perīculō aliēnō sapit.
Who becomes wise through someone else's difficulties
becomes wise in a happy fashion.
(*Plautus*, Mercator 4.7.40)

406

Irācundiam quī vincit, hostem superat maximum.
Who conquers anger conquers his greatest enemy.
(*Publilius Syrus*, 251)

407

Nōn omnēs quī habent citharam sunt citharoedī.
Not all people who have a lyre are lyre players.
(*Varro*, De Re Rustica, 2.1.3)

408
Improbē Neptūnum accūsat
quī iterum naufrāgium facit.
Who suffers a shipwreck a second time
unjustly accuses Neptune.
(*Publilius Syrus*, Sententia 264)

Quod in nāvī gubernātor, quod in currū agitātor, quod in chorō praeceptor, quod dēnique lēx in cīvitāte et dux in exercitū, hoc Deus est in mundō.

What the helmsman is in a ship, what the driver is in a chariot, what the leader is in a chorus, and finally what law is in a state and a leader in the army, that is what God is in the world.

(Translation of Aristotle)

Sē damnat jūdex, innocentem quī opprimit.

The judge who punishes an innocent man condemns himself.

(Publilius Syrus, Sententia 614)

Male sēcum agit aeger, medicum quī hērēdem facit.

The sick man who makes his doctor his heir does himself a disservice.

(Publilius Syrus, Sententia 332)

Thēsaurum in sepulchrō pōnit, quī senem hērēdem facit.

Who makes an old man his heir puts his treasure in the grave.

(Publilius Syrus, Sententia 626)

413

Spīna etiam grāta est, ex quā spectātur rosa.

Even a thorn bush is pleasant, from which a rose is seen.

(*Publilius Syrus,* Sententia 610)

414

Ubī jūdicat quī accūsat, vīs, nōn lēx, valet.

Where the person who accuses is (also) the person who judges,
violence, not law, prevails.

(*Publilius Syrus,* Sententia 692)

415

Perīcla timidus etiam quae nōn sunt videt.

The timid person sees even dangers which do not exist.

(*Publilius Syrus,* Sententia 452)

416

Quot campō leporēs, tot sunt in amōre dolōrēs.

There are as many sorrows in love as there are rabbits in the field.

(*Medieval*)

417

Damnant quod nōn intellegunt.

They condemn what they do not understand.

(*Anonymous*)

418
Quī fugit molam, fugit farīnam.
Who runs away from the millstone, runs away from the flour.
If you don't work, you don't eat.
(Anonymous)

419
Stultus nīl cēlat: quod habet sub corde revēlat.
The stupid person conceals nothing: he reveals what he has in his heart.
(Medieval)

420
Vespere prōmittunt multī quod māne recūsant.
Many promise in the evening what they refuse the next morning.
(Medieval)

421
Occāsiō aegrē offertur, facile āmittitur.
Opportunity is presented rarely, and is easily lost.
(*Publilius Syrus*, Sententia 449)

422
Eget semper quī avārus est.
The person who is a miser is always in want.
(St. Jerome)

423

Nōn mē dērīdet quī sua facta videt.

The person who sees his own acts does not make fun of me.

(Anonymous)

424

Quot capita, tot sententia.

There are as many opinions as there are people.

(Anonymous)

425

Nīl agit exemplum lītem quod līte resolvit.

An example accomplishes nothing
that solves one controversy by introducing another.

(Horace, Satires 2.3.103)

426

Quam est fēlīx vīta quae sine odiīs trānsit!

How happy is a life which is spent without hatred!

(Pubilius Syrus, Sententia 547)

427

Nōn bene olet quī bene semper olet.

A person does not smell good who always smells good.

(Martial, 2.12.4)

428
Crēscit avāritia quantum crēscit tua gaza.
Greed increases as much as your money increases.
(Medieval)

429
Quod vērum, tūtum.
What is true, is safe.
(Anonymous)

430
Quī capit uxōrem, lītem capit atque dolōrem.
Who takes a wife, takes trouble and strife.
(Medieval)

431

Omnia... habet quī nihil concupīscit.

Who desires nothing has everything.
(*Valerius Maximus*, Facta et Dicta Memorabilia 4.4.1)

432

Male agitur cum dominō quem vīlicus docet.

It goes badly with a master whom the foreman instructs.
(*Anonymous*)

433

Quidquid fit cum virtūte, fit cum glōriā.

Whatever is done with courage is done with glory.
(*Publilius Syrus*, Sententia 538)

434

Sub nive quod tegitur, dum nix perit, omne vidētur.

Everything which is covered by snow appears when the snow disappears.
(*Medieval*)

435

Nec temere nec timidē.

Neither rashly nor timidly.
(*Family motto*)

436

Nōn est vir fortis ac strēnuus quī labōrem fugit.
The person who runs away from hard work is not a brave and active man.
(*Seneca*, Epistulae Morales 22.7)

437

Quālis dominus, tālis et servus.
As the master is, so is the servant.
(*Petronius*, Satyricon 58)

438

Fēlīx, quem faciunt aliēna perīcula cautum.
Happy is the person whom other people's dangers make cautious.
(*Medieval*)

439

Quem amat, amat; quem nōn amat, nōn amat.
Whom he likes, he likes; whom he does not like, he does not like.
(*Petronius*, Satyricon 37)

440

**Nōn omnis quī sapiēns dīcitur sapiēns
est, sed quī discit et retinet sapientiam.**
Not everyone who is called wise is wise,
but rather he who learns and retains wisdom.
(*Petrus Alphonsus*, Disciplina Clericalis 2 [de silentio] p. 8)

441

Quī capit, capitur.

Who captures is himself captured.

(Anonymous)

442

Nēmō malus quī nōn stultus.

There is no bad person who is not foolish.

A person desires evil only because he foolishly thinks it is good.
(Robert Burton, 1577–1640, English writer
and author of The Anatomy of Melancholy)

443

Citō fit, quod dī volunt.

What the gods want comes to pass quickly.

(Petronius, Satyricon 76)

444

Semper inops quīcumque cupit.

Whoever desires is always poor.

(Claudius Claudianus, In Rufinium 1.200)

445

Dat virtūs quod forma negat.

Virtue gives what beauty denies.

(Motto)

446
Nēmō me impūne lacessit.
No one attacks me with impunity.
(Motto of Black Watch)

447
Quī parcē sēminat, parcē et metit.
Who sows sparingly also reaps sparingly.
(Paul, 2 Corinthians 9.6 [St. Jerome's Vulgate translation])

448
Quī sua perpendit, mea crīmina nōn reprehendit.
Who weighs his own faults does not condemn mine.
(Medieval)

449
Ōs, oculus, vultus prōdunt quod cor gerit intus.
The mouth, the eyes, the expression betray what the heart has inside.
(Medieval)

450
**Quod in juventūte nōn discitur,
in mātūrā aetāte nescītur.**
What is not learned in one's youth is not known at a mature age.
(Cassiodorus, Variae 1.24)

451

Bonum quod est supprimitur, numquam exstinguitur.

What is good is suppressed, but never extinguished.

(*Publilius Syrus,* Sententia 63)

452

Suum cuique pulchrum est.

One's own seems handsome to each person.

(*M. Tullius Cicero,* Tusculanae Disputationes 5.22.63)

453

Mortuō leōnī et leporēs īnsultant.

Even rabbits insult a dead lion.

(*Anonymous*)

454

Fortī et fidēlī nihil difficile.

Nothing is difficult for the brave and faithful.

(*Motto*)

455

Rēgī et patriae fidēlis.

Faithful to king and country.

(*Motto*)

456

Cui Fortūna favet multōs amīcōs habet.

The person whom Fortune favors has many friends.

(Anonymous)

457

Homō hominī aut deus aut lupus.

For another human being, a human being is either a god or a wolf.

(Erasmus, 1466–1536, Dutch humanist, theologian, and scholar)

458

Inopiae dēsunt multa; avāritiae omnia.

Many things are lacking to poverty; everything is lacking to greed.

(Publilius Syrus, Sententia 236)

459

Taciturnitās stultō hominī prō sapientiā est.

For a stupid man silence is a substitute for wisdom.

(Publilius Syrus, Sententia 627)

460

Formīcae grāta est formīca, cicāda cicādae.

An ant is pleasing to an ant, and a grasshopper to another grasshopper.

(Translation of Theocritus, 310–250 BC, Idyll 9.31–32)

461

Rēx est quī metuit nihil, rēx est quīque cupit nihil; hoc rēgnum sibi quisque dat.

A king is a person who fears nothing, a king is a person who desires nothing; this kingdom each person gives himself.
(*Seneca*, Thyestes 388–390)

462

Nīl hominī certum est.

Nothing is sure for mankind.
(*Ovid*, Tristia 5.5.27)

463

Neque enim omnia Deus hominī facit.

For God does not do everything for mankind.
(*Seneca*, Naturales Quaestiones 7.30.3)

464

Nūlla fidēs inopī.

No faith is put in a person who does not have money.
(*Ausonius*, Epigrams 19.23.4)

465

Nihil difficile amantī.

Nothing is difficult for the lover.
(*M. Tullius Cicero*, Orator 10.33)

466

Nihil...semper flōret: aetās succēdit aetātī.

Nothing flourishes forever: one generation succeeds another generation.
(*M. Tullius Cicero*, Philippics 11.15.39)

467

Stat sua cuique diēs.

One's own day of death is set for each person.
(*Vergil*, Aeneid 10.467)

468

Deō fidēlis et Rēgī.

Faithful to God and King.
(*Motto*)

469

Īra perit subitō quam gignit amīcus amīcō.

Anger which one friend generates for another friend dies down quickly.
(*Medieval*)

470

Etiam īnstantī laesa repūgnat ovis.

Even a sheep, if it is injured, fights back against someone who threatens it.
(*Propertius*, 2.5.20)

471
Vulgōque vēritās jam attribūta vīnō est.
And now truth is commonly attributed to wine.
(*Pliny the Elder*, Naturalis Historia 14.141)

472
Summa sēdēs nōn capit duōs.
The highest position does not hold two people.
(*Anonymous*)

473
Quid caecō cum speculō?
What is the blind man doing with the mirror?
(*Medieval*)

474
Omne solum fortī patria est.
Every country is a native land for one who is brave.
(*Ovid*, Fasti 1.493)

475
Meus mihi, suus cuique est cārus.
Who is mine is dear to me,
who is someone else's is dear to him.
(*Plautus,* Captivi 400)

476
Tam dēest avārō quod habet quam quod nōn habet.
A miser lacks as much what he has as what he does not have.
(*Publilius Syrus,* Sententia 628)

477
Fortūnātō omne solum patria est.
For one who is happy, every country is a native land.
(*Anonymous*)

478
Adulātiō quam similis est amicītiae!
How similar to friendship is flattery!
(*Seneca,* Epistulae Morales 45.7)

479
Nūllus agentī diēs longus est.
No day is long for the person who is active.
(*Seneca,* Epistulae Morales 122.3)

480
Nīl agentī diēs longus est.
To one who does nothing the day is long.
(*Seneca? Apparently a misquote of the previous sentence*)

481

Cinerī glōria sēra venit.
Glory comes late to the ashes.
(*Martial,* 1.25.8)

482

Magnās inter opēs inops.
Poor in the midst of great riches.
(*Horace,* Odes 3.16.28)

483

Nūllī est hominī perpetuum bonum.
There is eternal prosperity for no man.
(*Plautus,* Curculio 189, *adapted*)

484

Dictum sapientī sat est.
A word to the wise is enough.
(*Plautus,* Persa 729)

485

Quot hominēs, tot sententia; suus cuique mōs.
There are as many opinions as there are men;
each one his own way of doing things.
(*Terence,* Phormio 454)

486
Sērō dat quī rogantī dat.
He gives late who gives to one who asks.
(Anonymous)

487
Mendācī, neque cum vēra dīcit, crēditur.
Belief is not given to a liar even when he tells the truth.
(M. Tullius Cicero, De Divinatio 2.71.146, *adapted)*

488
Cui dēest pecūnia, huic dēsunt omnia.
To whom money is lacking, to him all things are lacking.
(Anonymous)

489
Nūdum latrō trānsmittit;
etiam in obsessā viā pauperī pāx est.
The robber passes by the poor man;
even in a road that is besieged there is peace for the poor man.
(Seneca, Epistulae Morales 14.9)

490
Cuivīs dolōrī remedium est patientia.
Patience is a remedy for any grief you wish.
(Publilius Syrus, Sententia 96)

491

Aliēnum aes hominī ingenuō est servitūs.

For a free-born man, debt is a form of slavery.
(*Publilius Syrus*, Sententia 11)

492

Quod nimis miserī volunt, hoc facile crēdunt.

What unhappy people want too much, this they easily believe.
(*Seneca*, Hercules Furens 314–15)

493

Et latrō et cautus praecingitur ēnse viātor,
ille sed īnsidiās, hic sibi portat opem.

Both the highwayman and the cautious traveller are equipped with a sword,
but the former is carrying it as an ambush
and the latter is carrying it to assist himself.
(*Ovid*, Tristia 2.1.271)

494

Suī cuique mōrēs fingunt fortūnam.

A person's own way of life creates his fortune for him.
(*Cornelius Nepos*, Atticus 11.19)

495

Frēnōs impōnit linguae cōnscientia.

Conscience places reins upon our tongue.

(*Publilius Syrus,* Sententia 665)

496

Nōn mihī sapit quī sermōne sed quī factīs sapit.

As far as I am concerned, the person is not wise who is wise in his speech
but the person who is wise in his deeds.

(*Robert Burton, 1577–1640, English writer
and author of* The Anatomy of Melancholy)

497

Invidus omnis abest, sī prosperitās tibi nōn est.

Every envious person is absent, if you do not have prosperity.

(*Anonymous*)

498

Saepe subit poenās, ōrī quī nōn dat habēnās.

The person who does not put reins upon his mouth often suffers a penalty.

(*Medieval*)

499

Necessitātī quī sē accommodat sapit.

The person who accommodates himself to necessity is wise.

(*Anonymous*)

500

Mors omnibus īnstat.

Death threatens all.
(Common grave inscription)

501

Sōlitūdō placet Mūsīs, urbs est inimīca poētīs.

Solitude pleases the Muses, the city is unfriendly for poets.
(Petrarch)

502

Sōl omnibus lūcet.

The sun shines upon us all.
(Petronius, Satyricon 100)

503

Deus omnia nōn dat omnibus.

God does not give everything to everybody.
(Medieval)

504

Suus rēx rēgīnae placet.

Her own king pleases a queen.
(Plautus, Stichus 133)

505
Flamma fūmō est proxima.
Smoke is next to the fire.
(*Plautus*, Curculio 53)

506
Commūne naufragium omnibus est cōnsōlātiō.
A common shipwreck is a consolation for everybody.
(*Anonymous*)

507
Pūrīs omnia pūra.
To the pure all things are pure.
(*Paul,* Titus 1.15 *adapted* [*St. Jerome's Vulgate translation*])

508
Flūmen cōnfūsum reddit piscantibus ūsum.
The river which has been stirred up furnishes opportunity to fishermen.
(*Medieval*)

509
Alia aliīs placent.
Different things please different people.
(*Anonymous*)

510

Est puerīs cārus quī nōn est doctor amārus.

He who is not an unpleasant teacher is dear to children

(Medieval)

511

Fortibus est fortūna virīs data.

Fortune is given to brave men.

(Ennius, Annales 247)

512

Nihil amantibus dūrum est.

Nothing is difficult for lovers.

(St. Jerome, Epistulae 22.40)

513

Maximō perīclō custōdītur quod multīs placet.

That which is pleasing to many people is guarded with the greatest danger.

(Publilius Syrus, Sententia 326)

514

Vīs lēgibus inimīca.

Violence is hostile to the laws.

(Legal)

515
Vīcīna sunt vitia virtūtibus.
Vices are close to virtues.
(*St. Jerome,* Adversus Luciferem 15)

516
Deus superbīs resistit; humilibus autem dat grātiam.
God resists the proud, but grants grace to the humble.
(*Paul,* I Peter 5.5. *[St. Jerome's Vulgate translation]*)

517
Immodicīs brevis est aetās et rāra senectūs.
For those who are extraordinary, youth is short and old age uncommon.
(*Martial,* 6.29.7)

518
Nōn nōbīs sōlum.
Not for ourselves alone.
(*Motto*)

519
Jūstitia omnibus.
Justice for all.
(*Motto of District of Columbia*)

520
Fortūna favet fatuīs.
Fortune favors the stupid.
(Anonymous; A parody of "fortune favors the brave"?)

521
Deō, patriae, amīcīs.
For God, for country, for friends.
(Motto)

522
Aliud aliīs vidētur optimum.
Different things seem best to different people.
(Attributed to M. Tullius Cicero)

523
Illa placet tellūs in quā rēs parva beātum mē facit.
That land pleases me
in which a small piece of property makes me happy (or prosperous).
(Martial, 10.96.5–6)

524
Quod cibus est aliīs, aliīs est ācre venēnum.
What is food for some people is bitter poison for others.
(Anonymous)

525

Quī culpae īgnōscit ūnī, suādet plūribus.

Who forgives one fault, persuades more people to make similar errors.
(*Publilius Syrus*, Sententia 535)

526

Ingrāta sunt beneficia, quibus comes est metus.

Benefits are not welcome which are accompanied by fear.
(*Publilius Syrus*, Sententia 270)

527

Omnis enim rēs, virtūs, fāma, decus,
dīvīna hūmānaque pulchrīs dīvitiīs pārent.

For all things, virtue, fame, honor,
things divine and human, are obedient to beautiful riches.
(*Horace*, Satires 2.3.94–96)

528

Quisquis in vītā suā parentēs colit,
hic et vīvus et dēfūnctus deīs est cārus.

Whoever during his lifetime takes care of his parents,
this person both living and dead is dear to the gods.
(*Translation of Johannes Stobaeus*)

529
Nē Juppiter quidem omnibus placet.
Not even Jupiter is pleasing to everyone.
(Translation of Theognis)

530
Quod suāve est aliīs, aliīs est amārum.
What is pleasant for some is bitter for others.
(Anonymous)

531
Post naufragium maria temptantur.
The seas are tried after a shipwreck.
(Anonymous)

532
Longē fugit quisquis suōs fugit.
Whoever flees from his family flees a long way.
(Petronius, Satyricon 43)

533
Imperat aut servit collēcta pecūnia cuique.
Money which has been piled up either commands or obeys each person.
(Horace, Epistulae 1.10.47)

534
Quālis vir, tālis ōrātiō.
As a man is, so is his speech.
(*Anonymous*)

535
In tālī tālēs capiuntur flūmine piscēs.
In this kind of river these kinds of fish are caught.
(*Medieval*)

536
Quī tōtum vult, tōtum perdit.
Who wants all, loses all.
(*Anonymous*)

537
Quālis pater, tālis fīlius.
As the father is, so is the son. *Like father, like son; a chip off the old block.*
(*Anonymous*)

538
Aequore quot piscēs, fronde teguntur avēs, quot caelum stēllās, tot habet tua Rōma puellās.
As many fish as there are in the sea, as many birds as are covered by foliage, as many stars as the sky holds, so many girls does your Rome hold.
(*Ovid*, Ars Amatoria 1.58–59)

539

Quī genus jactat suum, aliēna laudat.

Who praises his own family, praises what belongs to others.
(*Seneca*, Hercules Furens 340–41)

540

Quot servī tot hostēs.

There are as many enemies as there are slaves.
(*Sextus Pompeius Festus*, p. 349)

541

Sapiēns quī prōspicit.

Wise is he who looks ahead.
(*Motto of Malvern College*)

542

Equī dōnātī dentēs nōn īnspiciuntur.

People do not look at the teeth of a horse which is given to them.
Don't look a gift horse in the mouth.
(*St. Jerome*, Epistulae ad Ephesios, [proemium])

543

Mēns et animus et cōnsilium et sententia cīvitātis posita est in lēgibus.

The mind and character and planning and feeling of the state lie in its laws.
(*M. Tullius Cicero*, Pro Cluentio 53.146)

544
Sīc trānsit glōria mundī.
Thus passes the glory of the world.
(Anonymous)

545
Sine doctrīnā vīta est quasi mortis imāgō.
A life without learning is like an image of death.
(Dionysius Cato, 3.1)

546
Silentium est sīgnum sapientiae et loquācitās est sīgnum stultitiae.
Silence is a sign of wisdom and talkativeness is a sign of stupidity.
(Petrus Alphonsus, Disciplina Clericalis 2 [de silentio] p. 8)

547
Bonae mentis soror est paupertās.
Poverty is the sister of an honest mind.
(Petronius, Satyricon 84)

548
Īgnōrantia lēgis nēminem excūsat.
Ignorance of the law excuses no one.
(Legal)

549

In cāsū extrēmae necessitātis omnia sunt commūnia.

In case of extreme necessity all things are in common.
(Legal)

550

Initium sapientiae timor Dominī.

Fear of God is the beginning of wisdom.
(Job 28.28 *[St. Jerome's Vulgate translation]*)

551

Quid est somnus gelidae nisi mortis imāgō?

What is sleep except the image of chilly death?
(*Ovid,* Amores 2.9.41)

552

Ex vitiīs alterīus sapiēns ēmendat suum.

From the faults of someone else the wise man corrects his own fault.
(*Publilius Syrus,* Sententia 150)

553

Bonus animus in malā rē dīmidium est malī.

In an evil situation a good frame of mind is half of the evil.
(*Plautus,* Pseudolus 452)

554
Dux vītae ratiō.
Reason is the leader of life.
(Latin equivalent of the motto of Phi Beta Kappa)

555
Magna vīs cōnscientiae.
The force of conscience is great.
(M. Tullius Cicero, Pro Milone 23.61; Tusculanae Disputationes 2.17.40)

556
Salūs populī suprēma lēx.
The safety of the people is the supreme law.
(Legal)

557
In nōmine Dominī incipit omne malum.
Every evil begins in the name of the Lord.
(Anonymous)

558
Rēgis amīcitia nōn est possessiō pūra.
The friendship of the king is not an ideal possession.
(Medieval)

559

Ōtium sine litterīs mors est et hominis vīvī sepultūra.

Leisure without learning is death and the burial of a living man.
(*Seneca*, Epistulae Morales 82.3)

560

Vōx populī vōx Deī.

The voice of the people is the voice of God.
(*Commonplace*)

561

Virtūtis amōre.

With love of virtue.
(*Motto*)

562

Rōma caput mundī.

Rome is the capital of the world.
(*Lucan*, Pharsalia 2.655, *adapted*)

563

Calamitās virtūtis occāsiō est.

Disaster is the opportunity for bravery.
(*Seneca*, De Providentia 4.6)

564
Īra initium insāniae.
Anger is the beginning of insanity.
(*Ennius*, fragment 438, *adapted*,
quoted by Cicero, Tusculanae Disputationes 4.23.52)

565
Prō lībertāte patriae.
For the freedom of my country.
(*Motto*)

566
Mūsica est mentis medicīna maestae.
Music is medicine for a sad mind.
(*Anonymous*)

567
Externus hostis maximum in urbe concordiae vinculum.
An enemy outside the city is the greatest bond of concord inside the city.
(*Anonymous*)

568
Index est animī sermō.
Talk is an indicator of the mind.
(*Medieval*)

569

Omnis ars nātūrae imitātiō est.

All art is an imitation of nature.
(*Seneca*, Epistulae Morales 65.3)

570

Crēscit amor nummī quantum ipsa pecūnia crēscit.

Love of money increases as much as money itself increases.
(*Juvenal*, Satires 14.139)

571

Metus enim mortis mūsicā dēpellitur.

For the fear of death is dispelled by music.
(*Censorinus*, Liber De Die Natali 12)

572

Contrā malum mortis nōn est medicāmentum in hortīs.

Against the evil of death there is no medicine in the gardens.
(*Medieval*)

573

Vīnum animī speculum.

Wine is the mirror of the mind.
(*Anonymous*)

574

Ūsus, magnus vītae magister, multa docet.
Experience, the great teacher of life, teaches us much.
(*M. Tullius Cicero*, Pro Rabirio Postumo 4.9, *adapted*)

575

Caput columbae, cauda scorpiōnis.
The head of a dove, the tail of a scorpion.
(*Bernard of Clairvaux, 1091–1153, French reformer of monastic life*)

576

Homō sine pecūniā mortis imāgō.
A man without money is an image of death.
(*Anonymous*)

577

Sermō datur cūnctīs, animī sapientia paucīs.
Speech is given to all, wisdom of mind to few.
(*Anonymous*)

578

**In nūllum avārus bonus,
sed in sē semper pessimus.**
The miser is good toward no one,
but toward himself he is always worst of all.
(*Publilius Syrus*, Sententia 234)

579
Causa paupertātis plērīsque probitās est.
For a good many people, the cause of their poverty is honesty.
(*Q. Curtius Rufus*, 4.1.20)

580
Satis ēloquentiae, sapientiae parum.
Enough eloquence, little wisdom.
(*Sallust*, Catiline 5.4)

581
Nullīus hospitis grāta est mora longa.
A long stay of no guest is pleasant.
(*Anonymous*)

582
Quī dēbet, līmen crēditōris nōn amat.
The person who owes
does not like the threshold of the person he owes money to.
(*Publilius Syrus*, Sententia 533)

583
Praemia virtūtis honōrēs.
Honors are the rewards for virtue.
(*School motto*)

584

Tempora praetereunt mōre fluentis aquae.

Times pass in the manner of running water.
(Medieval)

585

Amīcus animae dīmidium.

A friend is the half of one's soul.
(*St. Augustine,* Confessions 4.6, *adapted*)

586

Tot mundī superstitiōnēs quot caelō stēllae.

There are as many superstitions in the world as there are stars in the sky.
*(Robert Burton, 1577–1640, English writer
and author of* The Anatomy of Melancholy*)*

587

Pietās fundāmentum est omnium virtūtum.

Piety is the foundation of all the virtues.
(*M. Tullius Cicero,* Pro Plancio 12.29)

588

Injūriārum remedium est oblīviō.

The cure for injuries is forgetting about them.
(*Publilius Syrus,* Sententia 250)

589

Naufragium rērum est mulier malefīda marītō.

A woman faithless to her husband is a shipwreck of one's fortune.

(*Anonymous*)

590

Amīcus omnium, amīcus nūllōrum.

A friend of all is a friend of nobody.

(*Anonymous*)

591

Terrārum dea gentiumque, Rōma,
cui pār est nihil et nihil secundum.

Rome, goddess of earth and of people,
to whom nothing is equal and nothing is second.

(*Martial,* 12.8.1–2)

592

Perjūria rīdet amantum Juppiter.

Jupiter laughs at the lies of lovers.

(*Lygdamus,* 6.49–50 [*poems formerly attributed to Tibullus*])

593

Repetītiō est māter studiōrum.

Repetition is the mother of studies.

(*Anonymous*)

594

Distrahit animum librōrum multitūdō.

A great number of books distracts the mind.
(*Seneca*, Epistulae Morales 2.3, *adapted*)

595

Bis dat quī citō dat.

Who gives quickly gives twice.
(*Alciatus?*)

596

Stultōrum plēna sunt omnia.

Everything is full of foolish people.
(*M. Tullius Cicero*, Ad Familiares 9.22.4)

597

Domina omnium et rēgīna ratiō.

Reason is the mistress and queen of all.
(*M. Tullius Cicero*, Tusculanae Disputationes 2.21.47)

598

Ex ōre parvulōrum vēritās.

Truth out of the mouths of little children.
(*Anonymous*)

599

Māter artium necessitās.

Necessity is the mother of the arts.
(Anonymous)

600

Tōtus mundus deōrum est immortālium templum.

The whole world is the temple of the immortal gods.
(*Seneca*, De Beneficiis 7.7.3, *adapted*)

601

**Historia est testis temporum, lūx vēritātis,
vīta memoriae, magistra vītae, nūntia vetustātis.**

History is the witness of time, the light of truth,
the life of memory, the teacher of life, the messenger of antiquity.
(*M. Tullius Cicero*, De Oratore 2.36)

602

Sēditiō cīvium hostium est occāsiō.

Strife among the citizens is an opportunity for the enemy.
(*Publilius Syrus*, Sententia 621)

603

Amīcōrum sunt commūnia omnia.

All the possessions of friends are in common.
(*M. Tullius Cicero, Greek proverb quoted in* De Officiis 1.16.51)

604

Litterārum rādīcēs amārae, frūctūs dulcēs.

The roots of literary study are bitter, but the fruits are sweet.
(Ascribed to Cato by Diomedes)

605

In regiōne caecōrum, rēx est luscus.

In the country of the blind, the one-eyed is king.
(Erasmus, Adagia*)*

606

Cūrārum maxima nūtrix nox.

Night is the best nurse of cares.
(Ovid, Metamorphoses 8.81–2*)*

607

Rādīx omnium malōrum est cupīditās.

The root of all evil is greed.
(Paul, 1. Timothy 6.10 *[St. Jerome's Vulgate translation])*

608

Multōrum manibus grande levātur opus.

A heavy task is lightened by the hands of many.
(Anonymous)

609

Vir bonus est quis?
Quī cōnsulta patrum, quī lēgēs jūraque servat.

Who is the good man?
He who keeps the decrees of the Senate, who observes laws and justice.
(*Horace*, Epistulae 1.16.40–41)

610

Nihil rērum hūmānārum sine deī nūmine geritur.

Nothing in human affairs is carried out without the will of a god.
(*Cornelius Nepos*, Timoleon 4.3)

611

Maximum remedium īrae mora est.

Delay is the best remedy for anger.
(*Seneca*, De Ira 2.29.1)

612

Nōn recipit stultus verba prūdentiae.

The fool does not receive the words of wisdom.
(*Anonymous*)

613

Semper magnae fortūnae comes adest adulātiō.

Flattery is always the companion of good fortune.
(*P. Velleius Paterculus*, Historiae Romanae 2.102.3)

614

Discordia ōrdinum venēnum est urbis.

Discord between the classes is poison in a city.

(Anonymous)

615

Fallācēs sunt rērum speciēs.

The appearances of things are deceptive.

(Seneca, De Beneficiis 4.34)

616

Mors jānua vītae.

Death is the gateway to life.

(Anonymous)

617

**Scrīptōrum chorus omnis amat nemus
et fugit urbēs.**

All the chorus of the writers loves the woods and flees the cities.

(Horace, Epistulae 2.2.77)

618

Salūs cīvitātis in lēgibus sita est.

The safety of the state is placed in its laws.

(M. Tullius Cicero, In Verrem 2.1.4, *adapted*)

619

Crīmina quī cernunt aliōrum,
nōn sua cernunt.

Those who see the faults of others do not see their own faults.
(Anonymous)

620

Crux ancora vītae.

The cross is the anchor of life.
(Anonymous)

621

Deōrum dōna saepe nōn dōna.

The gifts of the gods are not always gifts.
(Anonymous)

622

Adulātiō, perpetuum malum rēgum.

Flattery, the perpetual evil for kings.
(Q. Curtius Rufus, 8.5.14, adapted)

623

Verbum Dominī manet in aeternum.

The word of God remains forever.
(Paul, I Peter 1:23 [St. Jerome's Vulgate translation])

624

Nōn vīribus aut vēlōcitāte aut celeritāte corporum rēs magnae geruntur sed cōnsiliō, auctōritāte, sententiā.
Great affairs are carried on not by strength or speed or swiftness of the body, but by plan, authority, and judgment.
(*M. Tullius Cicero*, De Senectute 17)

625

Lacrimae pondera vōcis habent.
Tears have the weight of a voice.
(*Ovid*, Heroides 3.4)

626

Nōn omnibus aegrīs eadem auxilia conveniunt.
The same remedies do not suit all sick people.
(*Celsus*, De Remediis 3.1.5)

627

Est pābulum animōrum contemplātiō nātūrae.
Contemplation of nature is food for the mind.
(*M. Tullius Cicero*, Academicae Quaestiones 127)

628

Nōmina stultōrum semper parietibus haerent.
Names of the stupid always cling to the walls.
(*Anonymous*)

629

Grātus animus est ūna virtūs, nōn sōlum maxima sed etiam māter virtūtum omnium reliquārum.

A grateful disposition is a unique virtue,
not only the greatest one but even the mother of all other virtues.
(*M. Tullius Cicero*, Pro Plancio 33.80)

630

Sōlem...ē mundō tollere videntur quī amīcitiam ē vītā tollunt.

Those who remove friendship from life
seem to take the sun from the world.
(*M. Tullius Cicero*, De Amicitia 23.47)

631

Septem hōrās dormīre satis juvenīque senīque.

Seven hours sleep is enough for young and old.
(*Medieval*)

632

Dulcis amor patriae, dulce vidēre suōs.

Sweet is love of country, sweet it is to see one's own family.
(*Anonymous*)

633

**Nōn quia difficilia sunt, nōn audēmus;
sed quia nōn audēmus, difficilia sunt.**

Not because things are difficult are we not bold;
but because we are not bold, things are difficult.
(*Seneca,* Epistulae Morales 104.26)

634

Errāre est hūmānum.

To err is human.
(*Anonymous*)

635

Anguillam caudā tenēs.

You are holding an eel by the tail.
(*Anonymous*)

636

Ars est cēlāre artem.

It is the function of art to conceal art.
(*Anonymous*)

637

Omnia scīre volunt omnēs, sed discere nōlunt.

Everybody wants to know everything, but they do not want to learn.
(*Medieval*)

638

Nec male olēre mihī nec bene olēre placet.

Neither smelling bad nor smelling good is pleasing to me.
(*Ausonius*, Epigrams 19.84.2)

639

Amāre et sapere vix deō concēditur.

To be in love and keep one's senses
is a thing which is hardly given to a god.
(*Publilius Syrus*, Sententia 22)

640

Dulce est dēsipere in locō.

It is pleasant to play the fool at the proper time and place.
(*Horace*, Odes 4.12.28)

641

Nescit nātūram mūtāre pecūnia pūram.

Money does not know how to change an incorrupt nature.
(*Medieval*)

642

Testis nēmō in suā causā esse dēbet.

No one ought to be a witness in his own case.
(*Legal*)

643

**Improbus est homō quī beneficium
scit accipere et reddere nescit.**

The man is wicked who knows how to receive a benefit
and does not know how to give one.

(*Plautus*, Persa 762)

644

Dum fēmina plōrat, dēcipere labōrat.

When a woman cries, she is trying to deceive.

(*Medieval*)

645

Quī timidē rogat docet negāre.

Who asks in a timid fashion is teaching the person he asks to refuse.

(*Seneca*, Phaedra 593–4)

646

Linguam compescere virtūs nōn est minima.

To hold one's tongue is a very great virtue.

(*Anonymous*)

647

Amāre simul et sapere ipsī Jovī nōn datur.

The ability to love and be wise at the same time is not given to Jupiter himself.

(*Anonymous*)

648

Fēlīx quī quod amat dēfendere fortiter audet.

Happy is he who dares to defend bravely that which he loves.
(Medieval)

649

**Ut ager quamvīs fertilis
sine cultūrā frūctuōsus esse nōn potest,
sīc sine doctrīnā animus.**

Just as a field, however fertile, cannot be fruitful without cultivation,
so the mind cannot be productive without education.
(*M. Tullius Cicero,* Tusculanae Disputationes 2.13)

650

**In malīs spērāre bene,
nisī innocēns, nēmō solet.**

No one, except an innocent person,
is accustomed to being optimistic in difficult circumstances.
(*Publilius Syrus,* Sententia 653)

651

Ōrāre est labōrāre.

Working is praying.
(Motto of Benedictine order)

652

Dīligere parentēs prīma nātūrae lēx.

The first law of nature is to love one's parents.
(*Valerius Maximus*, Facta et Dicta Memorabilia 5.4.7)

653

Difficile est trīstī fingere mente jocum.

It is hard to make a joke with a sad heart.
(*Lygdamus, 6.34 [poems formerly attributed to Tibullus]*)

654

Jūsta... ab injūstīs petere īnsipientia est.

It is foolishness to seek justice from the unjust.
(*Plautus*, Amphitruo 36)

655

Sī Deus prō nōbis, quis contrā nōs?

If God is for us, who is against us?
(*St. Paul*, Romans 8.31 [*St. Jerome's Vulgate translation*])

656

Male facere quī vult numquam nōn causam invenit.

A person who wants to do evil always finds reason.
(*Publilius Syrus*, Sententia 336)

657

Nec scīre fās est omnia.

It is not permitted to know everything.
(*Horace*, Odes 4.4.22)

658

Stultum facit Fortūna quem vult perdere.

Whom Fortune wishes to destroy she makes foolish.
(*Publilius Syrus*, Sententia 611)

659

Vitium est omnia crēdere, vitium nihil crēdere.

It is a mistake to believe everything, it is a mistake to believe nothing.
(*Pseudo-Seneca*)

660

Difficile est modum tenēre in omnibus.

It is difficult to keep moderation in everything.
(*St. Jerome*, Epistulae 108.20)

661

Aegrōtō dum anima est, spēs esse dīcitur.

While there is life in a sick person, there is said to be hope.
(*M. Tullius Cicero*, Ad Atticum 9.10.3)

662

Sine pennīs volāre haud facile est.
It is hard to fly without wings.
(Anonymous)

663

Hūmānum amāre est, hūmānum autem īgnōscere est.
It is human to love, it is human to forgive.
(Plautus, Mercator 319)

664

Scīre volunt omnēs; mercēdem solvere nēmō.
All wish to know; no one wishes to pay the price.
(Juvenal, Satires 7.157)

665

Quī tacet cōnsentīre vidētur.
Who is silent appears to give consent.
(Legal)

666

Jūris praecepta sunt: honestē vīvere, alterum nōn laedere, suum cuique tribuere.
These are the principles of law:
to lead a decent life, not to harm another, to give to each his own.
(Justinian, Institutes 1.1)

667

Nam et uxōrem dūcere et nōn dūcere malum est.

For it is a bad thing to marry and a bad thing not to marry.
(*Valerius Maximus,* Facta et Dicta Memorabilia 7.2.1, *adapted*)

668

**Rēx nōn dēbet esse sub homine sed sub Deō et lēge,
quia lēx facit rēgem.**

The king ought not to be under the influence of men but under the influence
of God and the law, because the law makes the king.
(*Henry Bracton, died 1268, attributed*)

669

Fraus est cēlāre fraudem.

It is dishonest to conceal dishonesty.
(*Anonymous*)

670

Perīculōsum est crēdere et nōn crēdere.

It is dangerous both to believe and not to believe.
(*Phaedrus, 3.10.1*)

671

Nec mortem effugere quisquam nec amōrem potest.

No one can escape either death or love.
(*Publilius Syrus,* Sententia 433)

672

Cattus amat piscem sed non vult tangere flumen.

The cat likes fish but does not want to touch the river.

(Medieval)

673

Est quaedam flēre voluptās.

To weep is a certain pleasure.

(Ovid, Tristia 4.3.37)

674

Ebrietās mōrēs aufert tibi, rēs et honōrēs.

Drunkenness takes away your character, your money, and your reputation.

(Medieval)

675

Nōn sentīre mala sua nōn est hominis, et nōn ferre, nōn est virī.

Not to feel one's misfortunes is not human,
and not to endure them is not manly.

(Seneca, De Consolatione ad Polybium 17)

676

Quī vult caedere canem, facile invenit fūstem.

Who wants to beat a dog, easily finds a stick.

(Anonymous)

677

Scīre lēgēs nōn est verba eārum tenēre sed vim ac potestātem.

Knowing the laws is not remembering their words,
but rather their force and power.

(Anonymous)

678

Legere et nōn intellegere est tamquam nōn legere.

To read and not understand is just like not reading.

(Anonymous)

679

Jūdicis est jūs dīcere, nōn dare.

It is the duty of the judge to explain the law, not to make it.

(Legal)

680

Aliud est cēlāre, aliud tacēre.

It is one thing to conceal, and something else to be quiet.

(Legal)

681

Stultitiam simulāre locō prūdentia summa est.

To pretend stupidity at the right time is the highest sort of prudence.

(Anonymous)

682

Cum...docēmus, discimus.

While we teach, we learn.

(Sergius)

683

Vincis cochleam tarditūdine.

You surpass the snail in slowness.

(Plautus, Poenulus 532)

684

Laudem virtūtis necessitātī damus.

We give praise of virtue to necessity.

(Quintilian, Institutio Oratoria 1.8.14)

685

Ex ōre tuō tē jūdicō.

I judge you from your own mouth.

(Anonymous)

686

Nec habeō nec careō nec cūrō.

I neither have, nor want, nor care.
(Motto)

687

Insānus mediō flūmine quaeris aquam.

You are insanely looking for water in the middle of the river.
(Propertius, 1.9.16)

688

Dum spīrō, spērō.

While I breathe, I hope.
(Motto)

689

Facile omnēs, cum valēmus,
rēcta cōnsilia aegrōtātīs damus.

We all, while we are well,
easily give good advice to the sick.
(Terence, Andria 309)

690

Elephantum ex mūre facis.

You are making an elephant out of a mouse.
(Anonymous)

691
Dum fāta fugimus, fāta stultī incurrimus.
While we flee fate, we foolishly run into the same fate we are trying to avoid.
(Robert Williams Buchanan, 1841–1901, English poet, novelist, and playwright)

692
Aliēna nōbīs, nostra plūs aliīs placent.
Other people's things please us, and our things please other people more.
(Publilius Syrus, Sententia 28)

693
Dīvitiae sunt causa malōrum.
Riches are the cause of evil.
(Anonymous)

694
Sōcratēs "Quam multa nōn dēsīderō!" inquit.
Socrates said, "How many things I do not want!"
(Anonymous)

695
Scrībimus indoctī doctīque.
We all write, learned and unlearned.
*(Robert Burton, 1577–1640, English writer
and author of* The Anatomy of Melancholy)

696

Audiō sed taceō.
I hear but I keep silent.
(*Motto*)

697

Cum īnfirmī sumus optimī sumus.
When we are sick, then we are the best.
(*Pliny the Younger*, Epistuae 7.26.1)

698

Cum ventīs lītigō.
I am fighting with the winds.
(*Petronius*, Satyricon 83)

699

Homō sum; hūmānī nīl ā mē aliēnum putō.
I am a human being; I consider nothing human alien to me.
(*Terence*, Heauton Timoroumenus 77)

700

Ibī potest valēre populus ubi lēgēs valent.
Where the laws are strong, there the people can be strong.
(*Publilius Syrus*, Sententia 291)

701

Dīvitiae meae sunt; tū dīvitiārum es.

My riches are mine; you belong to your riches.
(*Seneca*, De Vita Beata 22.5)

702

In eādem es nāvī.

You are in the same boat (as I am).
(*Anonymous*)

703

Stultum est timēre quod vītāre nōn potes.

It is foolish to fear what you cannot avoid.
(*Publilius Syrus*, Sententia 580)

704

Nam, sīve Graecō poētae crēdimus, aliquandō et īnsānīre jūcundum est.

If we believe the Greek poet,
sometimes it is pleasant even to take leave of our senses.
(*Seneca*, De Tranquillitate 17.10)

705

Facile cōnsilium damus aliīs.

We easily give advice to other people.
(*Robert Burton, 1577–1640, English writer
and author of* The Anatomy of Melancholy)

706

Deō servīre vēra lībertās.

Serving God is true liberty.

(Medieval)

707

**Aliquis nōn dēbet esse jūdex in propriā causā,
quia nōn potest esse jūdex et pars.**

No one ought to be judge in his own case,
because one cannot be both judge and participant.

(Legal)

708

Humilis nec altē cadere nec graviter potest.

The lowly person cannot fall far nor heavily.

(*Publilius Syrus*, Sententia 667)

709

Imperāre sibī maximum imperium est.

To be in control of one's self is the greatest control.

(*Seneca*, Epistulae Morales 113.30)

710

Nēmō omnia potest scīre.

No one can know everything.

(*Varro*, De Re Rustica 2.1.2)

711

Beneficium accipere lībertātem est vendere.

To accept a benefit is to sell one's liberty.
(*Publilius Syrus,* Sententia 48)

712

Fortis cadere, cēdere nōn potest.

The brave person can fall but he cannot yield.
(*Family motto*)

713

Supplicem hominem opprimere,
virtūs nōn est sed crūdēlitās.

To punish a man who is asking for mercy is not courage but cruelty.
(*Publilius Syrus,* Sententia 682)

714

Nūdō dētrahere vestīmenta quis potest?

Who is able to take clothes away
from a person who does not have any clothes?
(*Plautus,* Asinaria 92)

715

Nec piscātōrem piscis amāre potest.

The fish cannot love the fisherman.
(*Robert Burton, 1577–1640, English writer
and author of* The Anatomy of Melancholy)

716

Amantēs dē formā jūdicāre nōn possunt.

Lovers cannot judge about beauty.
*(Robert Burton, 1577–1640, English writer
and author of* The Anatomy of Melancholy*)*

717

Labōribus vendunt deī nōbīs omnia bona.

The gods sell us everything at the price of our labor.
(Anonymous)

718

Juvenīle vitium est regere nōn posse impetūs.

It is a youthful fault not to be able to control one's impulses.
(Seneca, Troades 250)

719

Nōn potest arbor bona frūctūs malōs facere neque arbor mala frūctūs bonōs facere.

A good tree cannot bring forth bad fruit
nor can a bad tree bring forth good fruit.
(Matthew 7.18 [*St. Jerome's Vulgate translation*])

720

Rem āctam agis.

You are doing something which has been done before.
(Plautus, Pseudolus 260)

721

Vitia nostra regiōnum mūtātiōne nōn fugimus.

We do not flee our vices by changing our location.

(Anonymous)

722

Dum bibimus, dum serta, unguenta, puellās poscimus, obrēpit nōn intēllēcta senectūs.

While we drink, while we ask for garlands, ointments, and girls, old age creeps up on us undiscovered.

(Juvenal, Satires 9.128–9)

723

Est profectō Deus, quī quae nōs gerimus auditque et videt.

There certainly is a God, who sees and hears what we do.

(Plautus, Captivi 313)

724

Eripere vītam nēmō nōn hominī potest, at nēmō mortem.

Everyone can take away a man's life, but no one can take away his death.

(Seneca, Phoenissae 152–3)

725

Fortūna opēs auferre, nōn animum, potest.

Fortune can take away your wealth, but not your soul.
(*Seneca*, Medea 176)

726

Mediīs sitiēmus in undīs.

We will be thirsty in the middle of the water.
(*Ovid*, Metamorphoses 9.761)

727

Nōn ergō fortūnā hominēs aestimābō sed mōribus; sibī quisque dat mōrēs, condiciōnem cāsus assīgnat.

I will not therefore estimate men according to their fortune
but according to their character;
each person gives himself his character
but chance assigns us our status in life.
(*Macrobius*, Saturnalia 1.11.10)

728

Sum quod eris.

I am what you will be.
(*Tombstone inscription*)

729

Nōn sī male nunc et ōlim sīc erit.

If things are bad now, they will not be this way at some time in the future.
(*Horace,* Odes 2.10.17–18)

730

Dabit īra vīrēs.

Anger will give strength.
(*Seneca,* Troades 672)

731

Populus...quī dabat ōlim imperium, fascēs, legiōnēs, omnia, nunc sē continet atque duās tantum rēs anxius optat, pānem et circēnsēs.

The Roman people who once gave military command, the fasces,
legions, and everything, now restrain themselves
they only anxiously hope for two things, bread and circuses.
(*Juvenal,* Satires 10.74–81)

732

Hodiē nūllus, crās maximus.

Today no one, tomorrow the mightiest.
(*Anonymous*)

733

Labōre vincēs.
You will conquer by hard work.
(Family motto)

734

Post trēs saepe diēs vīlēscit piscis et hospes.
After three days a fish and a guest often start to go bad.
(Medieval)

735

Sī caecus caecum dūcit, ambō in foveam cadunt.
If one blind man leads another, both fall into the pitfall.
The blind leading the blind.
(Anonymous)

736

Dīligēs Dominum Deum tuum, ex tōtō corde tuō et proximum tuum sīcut tē ipsum.
Thou shalt love the Lord thy God with all thy heart,
and thy neighbor as thyself.
(Luke 10:27 [St. Jerome's Vulgate translation])

737

Animō imperābit sapiēns, stultus serviet.
The wise man will command his emotions, the foolish man will obey them.
(Publilius Syrus, Sententia 41)

738

Contuméliam sī dīcēs, audiēs.

If you say abusive things to others, you will hear abusive things in return.

(*Plautus,* Pseudolus 1173)

739

Vitia erunt dōnec hominēs.

There will be vices as long as there are men.

(*Tacitus,* Histories 4.74)

740

Hodiē, nōn crās.

Today, not tomorrow.

(*Motto*)

741

In sūdōre vultūs tuī comedēs pānem tuum.

In the sweat of thy brow shalt thou eat thy bread.

(Genesis 3:19 [*St. Jerome's Vulgate translation*])

742

Magna est vēritās et praevalēbit.

Great is truth and it will prevail.

(*Anonymous*)

743

Quī quae vult dīcit quae nōn vult audiet.

Who says what he wants will hear what he does not want.
(*Terence*, Andria 920)

744

Servābō fidem.

I will keep the faith.
(*Family motto*)

745

Jūstus ut palma flōrēbit.

The just will flourish as the palm tree.
(Psalms 91(92):13 [*St. Jerome's Vulgate translation*])

746

Laetus sorte tuā vīvēs sapienter.

If you are happy with your fortune, you will live wisely.
(*Anonymous*)

747

Nūllus ad āmissās ībit amīcus opēs.

No friend will come to riches which have been lost.
(*Ovid*, Tristia 1.9.10)

748

Catō contrā mundum.
Cato against the world.
(Anonymous)

749

Caecus caecō dux.
The blind man is the leader for the blind.
(Medieval)

750

Rēx erat Ēlisabeth, nunc est rēgīna Jacōbus.
Our king was Elizabeth, now our queen is James.
(Anonymous)
Elizabeth was a strong ruler and her successor, James I, (James VI of Scotland), son of Mary Queen of Scots, was weak and unpopular.

751

Quī amat perīculum in illō perībit.
Who loves danger will die in danger.
(Anonymous)

752

Is quī bibit hanc aquam, sī fidem addit, salvus erit.
He who drinks this water will be cured if he adds faith.
(Seen at famous spas)

753

Deus mihī prōvidēbit.

God will provide for me.
(Family motto)

754

Nōn semper erit aestās.

It will not always be summer.
(Anonymous)

755

Quō nōn ascendam?

Where will I not climb?
(Family motto)

756

Quod hodiē nōn est, crās erit.

What does not happen today will happen tomorrow.
(Petronius, Satyricon 45)

757

Arborēs serit dīligēns agricola, quārum aspiciet bācam ipse numquam:
vir magnus lēgēs, īnstitūta, rem publicam nōn seret?

The diligent farmer plants trees whose fruit he will never see:
will not a great man plant laws, institutions, and a state
(*M. Tullius Cicero,* Tusculanae Disputationes 1.14.31)

758

Intima cognōscēs per mōrēs exteriōrēs.

You will perceive innermost thoughts by external actions.
(*Medieval*)

759

Vulpēs saepe viam per vītēs invenit aptam.

A fox often finds a good path through the vines.
(*Medieval*)

760

Hodiē ille, crās egō.

He (lies in the grave) today, I (will lie in one) tomorrow.
(*Grave inscription*)

761

Omnia quae tua sunt post mortem nīl tibi prōsunt.

Everything which is yours will be of no advantage to you after your death.

(Anonymous)

762

Turbā muscārum fortis cōnfunditur ursus;
Trōjam nōn poterat dēvincere sōlus Ulīxēs.

A brave bear is disturbed by a swarm of flies;
Ulysses was not able to conquer Troy by himself.

(Medieval)

763

Nātūra...sēmina nōbīs scientiae dedit;
scientiam nōn dedit.

Nature has given us the seed of knowledge; she has not given us knowledge.

(Seneca, Epistulae Morales 120.4)

764

Ēripuit caelō fulmen scēptrumque tyrannīs.

He has taken the thunderbolt from the sky and the sceptre from the tyrants.

(Anne Robert Jacques Turgot, Baron de l'Auline, 1727–1781,
French statesman and economist)

765

Egō sum rēx Rōmānus et suprā grammaticam.

I am a Roman king and above grammar.

(King Sigismund the First?)

766

Nūllum magnum ingenium sine mixtūrā dēmentiae fuit.

There has been no great genius without a mixture of madness.

(*Seneca*, De Tranquillitate 17.10)

767

Incidit in foveam quam fēcit.

He falls into the pit which he dug himself.

(Anonymous)

768

Nec quae praeteriit iterum revocābitur unda, nec quae praeteriit hōra redīre potest.

The river which has passed by will never be called back, and the hour which has passed can never return.

(*Ovid*, Ars Amatoria 3.63–64)

769

Nōn ego sum stultus, ut ante fuī.

I am not as foolish as I was before.

(*Ovid*, Amores 3.11.32)

770

Levis est Fortūna: citō reposcit quod dedit.

Fortune is fickle: she quickly demands the return of what she has given.
(Publilius Syrus, Sententia 295)

771

Nūllum quod tetigit nōn ōrnāvit.

He adorned everything which he touched.
(Oliver Goldsmith's epitaph written by Samuel Johnson)

772

Afflāvit Deus et dissipantur.

God caused the storm and they are scattered.
(Motto on medal commemorating defeat of Spanish Armada)

773

Odimus quem laesimus.

We hate a person whom we have hurt.
(Anonymous)

774

Lāta porta et spatiōsa via quae dūcit ad perditiōnem, et multī sunt quī intrant per eam.

Broad is the gate and wide the road which leads to destruction, and there are many who enter through it.
(Matthew 7.13 [St. Jerome's Vulgate translation])

775
Quī per virtūtem periit...nōn interit.
The person who perishes through courage does not die.
(*Plautus,* Captivi 690)

776
Flet victus, victor interiit.
The conquered person weeps, the victor has died.
(*Anonymous*)

777
Deus dedit, Deus abstulit.
God has given, God has taken away.
(Job 1.21 [*St. Jerome's Vulgate translation*])

778
Nē Herculēs quidem contrā duōs.
Not even Hercules can do anything against two people.
(*Anonymous*)

779
Nōn obiit, abiit.
The dead person has not perished, but just gone away.
(*Grave inscription*)

780
Quī plantāvit cūrābit.
The person who has planted something will care for it.
(Theodore Roosevelt, 1858–1919, Twenty-sixth President of the United States)

781
Minimum ēripit Fortūna cum minimum dedit.
Fortune takes away the least from you when she has given you the least.
(Anonymous)

782
Amor ōdit inertēs.
Cupid hates the lazy.
(Ovid, Ars Amatoria 2.229)

783
Et servī hominēs sunt et aequē ūnum lactem bibērunt, etiam sī illōs malus fātus oppressit.
Slaves are human beings too, and they drink one kind of milk
just like ourselves, even if a bad fate has oppressed them.
(Petronius, Satyricon 71.1)

784

Odērunt hilarem trīstēs, trīstemque jocōsī,
sēdātum celerēs, agilem gnāvumque remissī.

Gloomy people hate the person who is cheerful,
and those who are jolly hate the gloomy one, the quick hate the person
who sits around, and those who are lazy hate an active and busy person.

(*Horace,* Epistulae 1.18.89–90)

785

Capitur urbs quae tōtum cēpit orbem.

The city which captured the whole world is now captured.

(*Attributed to St. Jerome*)

786

Nārrātis quod nec ad caelum nec ad terram pertinet.

You say what pertains neither to heaven nor to earth.

(*Petronius,* Satyricon 44, *adapted*)

787

Habeō senectūtī magnam grātiam, quae mihī
sermōnis aviditātem auxit, pōtiōnis et cibī sustulit.

I am much obliged to old age, which has increased my desire for talk
and removed the desire for drink and food.

(*M. Tullius Cicero,* De Senectute 14.46)

788
Nēminem pecūnia dīvitem fēcit.
Money has made no one rich.
(*Seneca,* Epistulae Morales 119.9)

789
Quī extrēmum rīsit optime rīsit.
Who laughed last laughed best.
(*Anonymous*)

790
Numquam, ubī diū fuit ignis, dēficit vapor.
When there has been a fire for a long time, the smoke is never lacking.
(*Anonymous*)

791
Multī multa, nēmō omnia nōvit.
Many know many things, no one knows everything.
(*Anonymous*)

792
Dominus dedit.
The Lord has given.
(*Motto of Lord Herries*)

793

Dīmidium factī quī coepit habet.
Who has begun has half the job done.
(*Horace*, Epistulae 1.2.40)

794

Fortūnātus et ille deōs quī nōvit agrestēs.
Happy is he who knows the rural divinities.
(*Vergil*, Georgics 2.493)

795

Bonīs nocet quisquis pepercit malīs.
Whoever has spared evil people harms good people.
(*Anonymous*)

796

Vērus amor nūllum nōvit habēre modum.
True love does not know how to observe moderation.
(*Propertius*, 2.15.30)

797

Per nūllam sortem poteris dēpellere mortem.
Through no fortune can you avoid death.
(*Medieval*)

798

Quod nēmō nōvit paene nōn fit.

What no one knows almost does not occur.

(*Apuleius*, Metamorphoses 10.3—*also known as* The Golden Ass)

799

Fēlīx quī potuit rērum cognōscere causās atque metūs omnēs et inexōrābile fātum subjēcit pedibus.

Happy is he who was able to learn the reason for things and put all fears and implacable fate under his feet.

(*Vergil*, Georgics 2.490–492)

800

Quī parcit virgae ōdit fīlium suum.

Who spares the rod hates his child.

(Proverbs 13.24 [*St. Jerome's Vulgate translation*])

801

Adam prīmus homō damnāvit saecula pōmō.

Adam, the first man, damned the centuries with the fruit.

(*Medieval*)

802

Beāta mors quae ad beātam vītam aditum aperit.

Blessed is death which opens the door to blessed life.

(*Robert Burton, 1577–1640, English writer and author of* The Anatomy of Melancholy)

167

803
Christiānōs ad leōnem!
To the lions with the Christians!
(*Tertullian,* Apology 40.2)

804
Hoc fuit, est, et erit: similis similem sibi quaerit.
This was true, is true, and will be true:
a person seeks someone who is like himself.
(*Medieval*)

805
Contemnunt spīnās cum cecidēre rosae.
They despise the thorns when the roses have fallen.
(*Ovid,* Fasti 5.354, *adapted*)

806
Quī sēsē accūsat ipse, ab aliō nōn potest.
Who accuses himself cannot be accused by someone else.
(*Publilius Syrus,* Sententia 672)

807
Nōn sibī sed patriae.
Not for one's self but for one's country.
(*Family motto*)

808
Rīsus sine causā abundat in ōre stultōrum.
Laughter without any reason behind it is common in the mouths of the stupid.
(Anonymous)

809
Suāviter in modō, firmiter in rē.
Gentle in how we do it, firm in what we do.
(Motto of Lord Newborough)

810
Formōsōs saepe invēnī pessimōs,
et turpī faciē multōs cognōvī optimōs.
I have often discovered beautiful people to be the worst,
and I have discovered many fine people with unpleasant appearance.
(Phaedrus, 3.4.6–7)

811
Graecia capta ferum victōrem cēpit.
Conquered Greece captured her savage victor.
(Horace, Epistulae 2.1.156)

812
Bonus jūdex damnat improbanda, nōn ōdit.
A good judge condemns what is wrong, but he does not hate it.
(Seneca, De Ira 1.16.6)

813

Intrā fortūnam dēbet quisque manēre suam.
Each person ought to stay within his own fortune.
(*Ovid*, Tristia 3.4.25–26)

814

Quī amant ipsī sibi somnia fingunt.
Lovers create dreams for themselves.
(*Anonymous*)

815

Frīgiditās hiemis, vēris lascīvia,
fervor aestātis studium surripuēre mihī.
The coldness of winter, the riot of spring,
the heat of summer have taken away from me the desire for study.
(*Medieval*)

816

Quī sibi nōn parcit, mihi vel tibi quō modō parcet?
How will he spare either you or me, who does not spare himself?
(*Medieval*)

817

Nēmo sibī satis est; eget omnis amīcus amīcō.
No one is sufficient unto himself; every friend needs a friend.
(*Medieval*)

818

Vir sapiēns, quī sē ad cāsūs accommodat omnēs.

It is a wise man who adapts himself to all situations.
(Medieval)

819

Nōn facit hoc aeger quod sānus suāserat aegrō.

When a person is sick, he does not do
what he persuaded his sick friend to do when he himself was healthy.
(Medieval)

820

Quidquid superī voluēre perāctum est.

Whatever the gods wanted is accomplished.
(Ovid, Metamorphoses 8.619)

821

In nūllum avārus bonus est, in sē pessimus.

The greedy man is good to no one, but toward himself he is the worst.
(Publilius Syrus, Sententia 234)

822

Ūnus erat mundus. "Duo sunt," ait ille: fuēre.

There was one world. Columbus said, "There are two." And there were.
(Inscription at Columbus' birthplace)

823

**Est homo rēs fragilis, nōn dūrāns tempore longō;
est ergō similis flōrī, quī crēscit in agrō.**

Man is a fragile thing, not lasting for a long time;
he is therefore similar to the flower which grows in the field.

(Medieval)

824

Indīgnē vīvit per quem nōn vīvit alter.

A person lives an unworthy life,
through whose efforts someone else does not live.

(Anonymous)

825

Omnis quī ōdit frātrem suum homicīda est.

Everyone who hates his brother is a murderer.

(I John 3.15 *[St. Jerome's Vulgate translation]*)

826

Amīcī, diem perdidī.

Friends, I have lost a day.

(Suetonius, Titus 8.1)

827

Quī fert malīs auxilium post tempus dolet.

Who helps evil people later has cause for grief.
(*Phaedrus*, 4.20.1)

828

**Quem diēs vīdit veniēns superbum,
hunc diēs vīdit fugiēns jacentem.**

What person in haughty mood the rising sun has seen,
this person the sinking sun has seen lying prostrate.
(*Seneca*, Thyestes 613–614)

829

Habet apud malōs quoque multum auctōritātis virtūs.

Among evil persons too, virtue has much authority.
(*Quintilian*, Declamationes Maiores 253)

830

Quod potuī perfēcī.

What I was able to do, I did to perfection.
(*Motto of Viscount Melville*)

831

Cujus est solum, ejus est ūsque ad caelum.

Whoever owns the ground owns all the way to the heavens.
(*Legal*)

832

Quī timet Deum, omnia timent eum;
quī vērō nōn timet Deum, timet omnia.

All things are afraid of the person who is afraid of God;
but the person who is not afraid of God is afraid of everything.
(*Petrus Alphonsus,* Disciplina Clericalis Prologue (de timore Dei) p. 1)

833

Quī omnēs īnsidiās timet in nūllās incidit.

Who is afraid of all ambushes falls into none.
(*Publilius Syrus,* Sententia 542)

834

Sat citō sī sat bene.

Done quickly enough if done well enough.
(*Cato in Aulus Gellius,* Attic Nights 16.14)

835

Arbore dējectā, quī vult ligna colligit.

When a tree has been blown down, whoever wants the wood collects it.
(*Anonymous*)

836

Fortūna immoderāta in bonō aequē atque in malō.

Fortune is unrestrained equally in good and in bad.

(*Laberius, ca. 106–43 BC*)

837

Speculātor adstat dēsuper, quī nōs diēbus omnibus āctūsque nostrōs prōspicit.

A watchman stands above, who looks at us and our actions every day.

(*Anonymous*)

838

Saepe dat ūna diēs quod tōtus dēnegat annus.

Often one day gives what an entire year has denied.

(*Medieval*)

839

Ferē libenter hominēs id quod volunt crēdunt.

Generally people gladly believe that which they want to believe.

(*Caesar*, Gallic War 3.18.2)

840

Grātia quae tarda est, ingrāta est grātia.

Gratitude which is expressed late is an ungrateful kind of gratitude.

(*Anonymous*)

841

Hoc faciunt vīna quod nōn facit unda marīna.

Wine does that which the waves of the sea do not.

(*Medieval*)

842

Perdit majōra quī spernit dōna minōra.

Who scorns smaller gifts loses the bigger gifts.

(Medieval)

843

Ignōscent, sī quid peccārō stultus, amīcī.

My friends will forgive me if I stupidly make an error.

(Horace, Satires 1.3.140)

844

Quī prior strīnxerit ferrum, ejus victōria erit.

Who first draws the sword, his will be the victory.

(Livy, Ab Urbe Condita 24.38)

845

Taurum tollet quī vitulum sustulerit.

Who has lifted the calf will lift the bull.

(Anonymous)

846

**Omnia nōvit Graeculus ēsuriēns;
ad caelum (jusseris) ībit.**

The hungry Greek knows everything; (if you order him) he will go to heaven.

(Juvenal, Satires 3.77–78)

847

Tenue est mendācium;
perlūcet, sī dīligenter īnspexeris.

A lie is thin; the light shines through if you look at it carefully.
(*Seneca,* Epistulae Morales 79.18)

848

Tē tua, mē mea dēlectant.

Your things please you, my things please me.
(*Anonymous*)

849

Fortūna per omnia hūmāna,
maximē in rēs bellicās, potēns.

In all human affairs, particularly in warfare, fortune is powerful.
(*Livy,* Ab Urbe Condita 9.17)

850

Omnia sub lēgēs mors vocat ātra suās.

Black death calls all things to her own jurisdiction.
(Consolatio ad Liviam 360 [*attributed to Ovid*])

851

Nāvita dē ventīs, dē taurīs nārrat arātor, et numerat mīles vulnera, pāstor ovēs.

The sailor talks about the winds, the plowman about his bulls, the soldier counts his wounds, and the shepherd counts his sheep.

(*Propertius*, 2.1.43–44)

852

Parva saepe scintilla contempta magnum excitāvit incendium.

Often a small, despised spark has created a large fire.

(*Q. Curtius Rufus*)

853

Multī ad fātum vēnēre suum, dum fāta timent.

Many come to their death while they fear fate.

(*Seneca*, Agamemnon 993–994)

854

Jūdex in propriīs est nūllus homō bonus āctīs.

No man is a good judge in his own affairs.

(*Medieval*)

855

Invidia, tamquam ignis, summa petit.
Envy, like fire, seeks the highest.
(*Livy*, Ab Urbe Condita 8.31)

856

Exitus ācta probat.
The end tests the undertaking.
(*Ovid*, Epistulae Ex Ponto 2.85)

857

Vīvit post fūnera virtūs.
Virtue lives after death.
(*Motto*)

858

Virtūte, nōn verbīs.
With courage, not with words.
(*Motto*)

859

Astra inclīnant sed nōn cōgunt.
The stars influence us but do not compel us.
(*Anonymous*)

860

Deum quaerēns gaudium quaerit.

Who seeks God seeks joy.

(Anonymous)

861

Socratēs prīmus philosophiam dēvocāvit ē caelō et in urbibus collocāvit et in domōs etiam intrōdūxit, et coēgit dē vītā et mōribus rēbusque bonīs et malīs quaerere.

Socrates was the first to call philosophy down from heaven and set it in the cities and even introduce it into our homes, and make it ask about daily life and customs and good and evil.

(M. Tullius Cicero, Tusculanae Disputationes 5.4.10)

862

Vēnit post multōs ūna serēna diēs.

After many days comes one sunny one.

(Lygdamus, 6.32 [poems formerly attributed to Tibullus])

863

Multōs morbōs multa fercula fēcērunt.

Many courses have created many diseases.

(Seneca)

864

Factum abiit, monumenta manent.

The deed has passed, the monuments remain.
(Motto of London Numismatic Society)

865

Fortūna omnia victōribus praemia posuit.

Fortune has presented all the rewards to the victors.
(Sallust, Catiline 20.14)

866

Nōn valet ēbrietās, per quam perit omnis honestās.

Drunkenness, through which all honor is lost, is no good.
(Medieval)

867

Vēritās ōdit morās.

Truth hates delays.
(Seneca, Oedipus 850)

868

Inopem mē cōpia fēcit.

Prosperity has made me poor.
(Ovid, Metamorphoses 3.466)

869

Quī medicē vīvit miserē vīvit.

Who lives a life run by doctors, lives an unhappy life.
(Anonymous)

870

Citharoedus rīdētur chordā
quī semper oberrat eādem.

The lyre player is laughed at who always makes a mistake on the same string.
(Horace, Ars Poetica 356)

871

Bis peccat quī crīmen negat.

He sins twice who denies his crime.
(Anonymous)

872

Frūstrā labōrat quī omnibus placēre studet.

Who tries to please everybody labors in vain.
(Anonymous)

873

**Mendācī hominī, nē vērum quidem dīcentī,
crēdere solēmus.**

We do not usually believe an untruthful man,
even when he is telling the truth.
(*M. Tullius Cicero*, De Divinatio 2.176)

874

**Sī Fortūna volet, fīēs dē rhētore cōnsul;
sī volet haec eadem, fīet dē cōnsule rhētōr.**

If Fortune wants, you will become a consul from being a rhetorician;
and if the same Fortune wishes,
you will become a rhetorician from being a consul.
(*Juvenal*, Satires 7.197–198)

875

Alta diē sōlō nōn est exstrūcta Corinthus.

Lofty Corinth was not built in a single day.
(*Anonymous*)

876

Dat pira, dat pōma, quī nōn habet altera dōna.

The person who does not have any other gifts gives pears and fruit.
(*Medieval*)

877

Faber est suae quisque fortūnae.

Each person is the creator of his own fortune.
(Appius Claudius Caecus)

878

Lītore quot conchae, tot sunt in amōre dolōrēs.

There are as many sorrows in love as there are shells on the seashore.
(*Ovid*, Ars Amatoria 2.519)

879

Corpora nostra lentē augēscunt, citō exstinguuntur.

Our bodies grow slowly but perish quickly.
(*Tacitus*, Agricola 3.1)

880

Inter caecōs rēgnat luscus.

Among the blind the one-eyed rules.
(Anonymous)

881

Fortūna numquam sistit in eōdem statū;
semper movētur; variat et mūtat vicēs,
et summa in īmum vertit ac versa ērigit.

Fortune never stands in the same place; she always moves;
she changes and varies her ways,
and turns the highest into low and raises up what has been overthrown.
(*Ausonius*)

882

Cottīdiē damnātur quī semper timet.

Who is always afraid is condemned every day.
(*Anonymous*)

883

Leve fit quod bene fertur onus.

The burden which is carried well becomes light.
(*Anonymous*)

884

Fēlīx quī nihil dēbet.

Happy is he who owes nothing.
(*Anonymous*)

885

Quisquis habet nummōs sēcūrā nāvigat aurā.

Whoever has money sails with a safe breeze.

(*Petronius*, Satyricon 137)

886

Quī bene amat bene castīgat.

Who loves well, chastises well.

(*Reflection of* Hebrews 12.6?)

887

Quālis rēx, tālis grex.

As the king is, so are the common people.

(*Robert Burton, 1577–1640, English writer
and author of* The Anatomy of Melancholy)

888

Nōn omne quod nitet aurum est.

Not everything which shines is gold.

(*Anonymous*)

889

Is est amīcus quī in rē dubiā rē juvat.

He is a friend who in a difficult situation assists you with material help.

(*Plautus*, Epidicus 113)

890

Spīna gerit flōrem, quae gignit tācta dolōrem.

The thorn which, when touched, produces pain, bears the flower.

(Anonymous)

891

**Paupertās est, nōn quae pauca possidet
sed quae multa nōn possidet.**

Poverty is not something which possesses few things
but which does not possess many things.

(Seneca, Epistulae Morales 87.39.1)

892

Cum grānō salis.

With a grain of salt.

(Anonymous)

893

Vōx clāmantis in dēsertō.

The voice of one crying in the desert.

(Matthew 3.3 *[St. Jerome's Vulgate translation]*)

894

Ecce Agnus Deī, quī tollit peccāta mundī.

Behold the Lamb of God, who takes away the sins of the world.

(I John, 29 *[St. Jerome's Vulgate translation]*)

895

Malī prīncipiī malus fīnis.
A bad end to a bad beginning.
(Anonymous)

896

Temeritās sub titulō fortitūdinis latet.
Rashness hides under the name of bravery.
(*Seneca*, Epistulae Morales 45.7)

897

Multī committunt eadem dīversō crīmina fātō; ille crucem sceleris pretium tulit, hic diadēma.
People commit the same crime with different results; one person gets the cross (crucifixion) as a reward for his evil, the other person gets a crown.
(*Juvenal*, Satires 13.103–105)

898

Magna est...vīs hūmānitātis.
The effect of a liberal education is great.
(M. Tullius Cicero)

899

Virtūtis praemium honor.
Honor is the reward for virtue.
(Motto)

900
Ex Āfricā semper aliquid novī.
From Africa there is always something new.
(*Pliny the Elder*, Naturalis Historia 8.17)

901
Frōns est animī jānua.
The forehead (face) is the doorway to the mind.
(*Quintus Tullius Cicero*)

902
Nīl prōdest oculus ā quō rēs nūlla vidētur.
The eye is not any good which does not see anything.
(*Medieval*)

903
Stat magnī nōminis umbra.
The shadow of a great name remains.
(*Lucan*, Pharsalia 1.135)

904
Quī dat beneficia deōs imitātur.
Who gives benefits imitates the gods.
(*Seneca*, De Beneficiis 3.15.4)

905

Nōn nōbīs sōlum nātī sumus.

We were not born only for ourselves.
(*M. Tullius Cicero*, De Officiis 1.7.22)

906

Homō totiēns moritur quotiēns āmittit suōs.

A man dies as often as he loses his family.
(*Publilius Syrus*, Sententia 215)

907

Rōma locūta est; causa fīnīta est.

Rome has spoken; the cause is finished.
(*Anonymous*)

908

Homō extrā corpus est suum cum īrāscitur.

A man is outside of his body when he is angry.
(*Publilius Syrus*, Sententia 204)

909

Poēta nāscitur, nōn fit.

A poet is born, not made.
(*Anonymous*)

910

Dormiunt aliquandō lēgēs, numquam moriuntur.
Sometimes the laws sleep, but they never die.
(Legal)

911

In tālī tālēs capiuntur flūmine piscēs.
In such a river are such fish caught.
(Medieval)

912

Poenam morātur improbus, nōn praeterit.
A wicked person delays his punishment; he does not escape it.
(Publilius Syrus, Sententia 478)

913

Mors fugācem persequitur virum.
Death follows after the man who flees [it].
(Horace, Odes 3.2.14)

914

**Saepe quod datur exiguum est;
quod sequitur ex eō, magnum.**
Often what is given is small, what follows from it is great.
(Seneca, Epistulae Morales 81.14)

915
Saepe mōrēs patris imitātur fīlius īnfāns.
Often a young son imitates the ways of his father.
(Medieval)

916
In bibliothēcīs loquuntur
dēfūnctōrum immortālēs animae.
Immortal spirits of the dead speak in libraries.
(Pliny the Elder, Naturalis Historia 35.2.9, *adapted)*

917
Rēx numquam moritur.
The king never dies.
(Legal)

918
Bonum quod est supprimitur, numquam exstinguitur.
What is good is suppressed but never extinguished.
(Publilius Syrus, Sententia 63)

919

Plērīque Deum vōcibus sequuntur, mōribus autem fugiunt.

Many follow God in their words but flee him in their actions.
(Othlonus)

920

Parturiunt montēs; nāscētur rīdiculus mūs.

The mountains are giving birth; a ridiculous mouse will be born.
(Horace, Ars Poetica 139)

921

Deum imitātur quī īgnōscit.

The person who pardons imitates God.
(Anonymous)

922

Honor sequitur fugientem.

Honor pursues the person who flees from it.
(Motto)

923

Ex malīs mōribus bonae lēgēs nātae sunt.

Good laws are born out of bad customs.
(Sir Edward Coke, 1552–1634, British jurist)

924

Saepe solet similis fīlius esse patrī.

A son is often accustomed to be like his father.
(Medieval)

925

"Omnēs" inquit Alexander "jūrant esse mē Jovis fīlium, sed vulnus hoc hominem mē esse clāmat."

Alexander said, "Everybody swears that I am the son of Jupiter,
but this wound declares that I am a man."
(*Seneca*, Epistulae Morales 59.12)

926

Amāns semper quod timet esse putat.

A lover always thinks that what he fears exists.
(*Ovid*, Ars Amatoria 3.720, *adapted*)

927

Ūnam virtūtem mīlle vitia comitantur.

A thousand faults accompany one virtue.
(*Robert Burton, 1577–1640, English writer
and author of* The Anatomy of Melancholy)

928

Nūlla fidēs pietāsque virīs quī castra sequuntur.
There is no faithfulness
and no pietās to men who [as hired soldiers] follow camps.
(*Lucan*, Pharsalia 10.407)

929

Nēmō doctus umquam... mūtātiōnem cōnsiliī incōnstantiam dīxit esse.
No educated person ever said that a change of plan was an inconsistency.
(*M. Tullius Cicero*, Ad Atticum 16.7.3)

930

Aegrōtātō dum anima est, spēs esse dīcitur.
While there is life for a sick person, hope is said to exist.
(*M. Tullius Cicero*, Ad Atticum 9.10.3)

931

Quisquis amat luscam, luscam putat esse venustam.
Whoever loves a one-eyed girl thinks the one-eyed girl is lovely.
(*Anonymous*)

932

Stultam fert mentem quī sē dīcit sapientem.
The person who says that he is wise reveals (*fert*) a stupid mind.
(*Medieval*)

933

Irātus, cum ad sē rediit, sibī tum īrāscitur.

When the angry man returns to himself, then he grows angry with himself.
(*Publilius Syrus,* Sententia 273)

934

Voluptātem maeror sequitur.

Sorrow follows pleasure.
(*Anonymous*)

935

Lēx ūniversa est quae jubet nāscī et morī.

It is a universal law which orders us to be born and to die.
(*Anonymous*)

936

Vēritās enim labōrāre potest, vincī non potest.

For truth can be in difficulty, [but] it cannot be conquered.
(*St. Jerome,* Ad Pelam 1.25)

937

Satis est beātus, quī potest cum vult morī.

He is happy enough who can die when he wishes.
(*Publilius Syrus,* Sententia 616)

938

Aliae nātiōnēs servitūtem patī possunt; populī Rōmānī est propria lībertās.

Other nations can endure slavery;
liberty belongs to (*propria est*) the Roman people.
(*M. Tullius Cicero*, Philippics 6.7.19)

939

Dīcīque beātus ante obitum nēmō suprēmaque fūnera dēbet.

No one ought to be called happy before his death and his last rites.
(*Ovid*, Metamorphoses 3.136–137)

940

Numquam est ille miser cui facile est morī.

Never is that person unhappy for whom it is easy to die.
(*Seneca*, Hercules Oetaeus 111)

941

Stultitia est timōre mortis morī.

It is stupidity to die for fear of death.
(*Seneca*, Epistulae Morales 70.8)

942

Ars prīma rēgnī est posse invidiam patī.
The first art of ruling is to be able to endure envy.
(*Seneca*, Hercules Furens 353)

943

Vēritās mūtārī nūllō modō potest.
Truth can change in no way.
(*Anonymous*)

944

Aut vincere aut morī.
Either to conquer or to die.
(*Anonymous*)

945

Ait omnia pecūniā efficī posse.
He says that everything can be accomplished by money.
(*M. Tullius Cicero*, In Verrem, *adapted*)

946

Nescit vōx missa revertī.
A word [once] released does not know how to return.
(*Horace*, Ars Poetica 390)

947

Dīves quī fierī vult et cito vult fierī.

Who wants to become rich also wants to become rich quickly.
(*Juvenal,* Satires 14.176)

948

Ei mihi! Difficile est imitārī gaudia falsa!

Alas! It is difficult to pretend false joys.
It is difficult to make a joke with a sad heart.
(*Lygdamus 3.6.33 [poems formerly attributed to Tibullus]*)

949

Nēmō dēbet bis vexārī prō ūnā et eādem causā.

No one ought to be persecuted twice for one and the same reason.
(*Legal*)

950

Quī nescit tacēre nescit et loquī.

He who does not know how to keep quiet does not even know how to speak.
(*Anonymous*)

951

In quattuor partēs honestum dīvidī solet: prūdentiam, jūstitiam, fortitūdinem, et temperantiam.

Honesty is generally divided into four parts:
prudence, justice, bravery, and moderation.
(*M. Tullius Cicero,* De Officiis 5, *adapted*)

952

Flectī potest, frangī nōn potest.

He can be bent, but he cannot be broken.
(*Motto*)

953

Quam miserum est mortem cupere nec posse ēmorī!

How miserable it is to desire death and not able to die.
(*Publilius Syrus,* Sententia 504)

954

Dē rē āmissā irreparābilī nē doleās.

You should not grieve about something which is irreplaceably lost.
(*Anonymous*)

955

Populus vult dēcipī: dēcipiātur.

The people wish to be deceived; let them be deceived.

(*Anonymous*)

956

Ōdit vērus amor nec patitur morās.
True love hates and does not suffer delays.
(*Seneca,* Hercules Furens 588)

957

Actum...nē agās.
Do not do what is already done. [Don't beat a dead horse.]
(*Terence,* Phormio 419)

958

Spērēmus quae volumus, sed quod acciderit ferāmus.
Let us hope for what we want, but let us endure whatever happens.
(*M. Tullius Cicero,* Pro Sestio 68.143)

959

Ignem ignī nē addās.
Do not add fire to fire.
(*Anonymous*)

960

Palmam quī meruit ferat.
Let him who has earned it carry away the palm.
(*Motto of Lord Nelson*)

961
Stet fortūna domūs.
Let the good fortune of this house remain.
(School motto)

962
Bibere hūmānum est; ergō bibāmus.
It is human to drink; therefore, let us drink.
(Rathskeller at Nuremburg)

963
Ante mortem nē laudēs hominem quemquam.
Do not praise any man before his death.
(Ecclesiastes 11.30 *[St. Jerome's Vulgate translation]*)

964
Pauper agat cautē.
The poor man should act cautiously.
(Anonymous)

965
Quid faciant lēgēs ubi sōla pecūnia rēgnat, aut ubi paupertās vincere nūlla potest?
What can laws do where money alone rules,
or where no poor man (poverty) can win?
(Petronius, Satyricon 14.2)

966

Ūnī nāvī nē committās omnia.

Do not entrust everything to one ship.

(Anonymous)

967

Sed ācta nē agāmus; reliqua parēmus.

Let us not do what has already been done; let us prepare for the rest.

(M. Tullius Cicero, Ad Atticum 9.6.7)

968

Vīvās!

May you live [in good health]!

(Roman toast)

969

Dētur glōria sōlī Deō.

Let glory be given to God alone.

(Motto)

970

Miserum est tacēre cōgī quod cupiās loquī.

It is wretched to be compelled to keep silent about that which you wish to say.

(Publilius Syrus, Sententia 314)

971

Haec...prīma lēx amīcitiae sānciātur, ut ab amīcīs honesta petāmus.

Let this first law of friendship be considered holy:
that we should seek honorable things from our friends.
(*M. Tullius Cicero,* De Amicitia 12.44)

972

Necesse est ut multōs timeat quem multī timent.

It is necessary that the person whom many fear should fear many people.
(*Psuedo-Publilius Syrus,* 217)

973

Edās, bibās ut bene vīvās; nōn vīvās ut tantum edās et bibās.

You should eat and drink in order to live a good life;
you should not live only to eat and drink.
(*Medieval*)

974

Sīmia sīmia est, etiam sī aurea gestet īnsīgnia.

A monkey is a monkey, even if he wears golden insignia.
(*Anonymous*)

975

Nisī per tē sapiās, frūstrā sapientem audiās.

Unless you are wise by yourself, you will listen to a wise man in vain.
(*Publilius Syrus*, Sententia 427)

976

Laetus sum laudārī ā laudātō virō.

I am happy to be praised by a man who has been praised.
(*M. Tullius Cicero*, Ad Familiares 5.12.7, *adapted*)

977

Nē tē submergās, cautē prope flūmina pergās.

In order not to drown, proceed cautiously near rivers.
(*Medieval*)

978

Sī cuculum doceās, nōn ejus cantica mūtās.

If you teach a cuckoo, you do not change his songs.
(*Medieval*)

979

Sufficit mihī cōnscientia mea; nōn cūrō quid dē mē loquantur hominēs.

My conscience is enough for me; I do not care what men say about me.
(*St. Jerome*, Epistulae 123.15)

980

Post trēs saepe diēs vīlēscit piscis et hospes, nī sale condītus vel sit speciālis amīcus.

After three days a fish and a guest often start to go bad unless (the fish is) preserved with salt or (the guest is) a very special friend.
(Medieval)

981

Vetus est enim lēx illa jūstae amīcitiae idem amīcī semper velint.

For it is an ancient law of just friendship that friends should always want the same thing.
(*M. Tullius Cicero*, Pro Plancio 2.5)

982

Nōn... dat nātūra virtūtem; ars est bonum fīerī.

Nature does not give virtue; it is an art to become something good.
(*Seneca*, Epistulae Morales 90.44)

983

Rem faciās, rem; sī possīs, rēctē; sī nōn, quōcumque modō rem.

Make money! Money! Honestly, if you can; if not, make money in whatever way [you can].
(*Horace*, Epistulae 1.1.65–66)

984

Hōrae quidem cēdunt et diēs et mēnsēs et annī;
nec praeteritum tempus umquam revertitur;
nec quid sequātur scīrī potest.

The hours indeed pass, and the days and the months and the years.
Nor does past time ever return; nor can what follows be known.
(*M. Tullius Cicero*, De Senectute 19.69)

985

Sī, quotiēns hominēs peccant, sua fulmina mittat
Juppiter, exiguō tempore inermis erit.

If Jupiter were to hurl his thunderbolts as often as men sin,
in a short time he would be unarmed.
(*Ovid*, Tristia 2.1.33–34)

986

Nescīs quid vesper sērus vehat.

You do not know what the late evening may bring.
(*Varro, quoted in Macrobius*, Saturnalia 1.7.12)

987

Immō, id quod ajunt, auribus teneō lupum. Nam neque
quō pactō ā mē dīmittam neque utī retineam sciō.

No, this is what they say: I am holding a wolf by the ears. For I don't know in
what way I can let it go from me nor how I can hold onto it.
(*Terence*, Phormio 506)

988

Prōnaque cum spectent animālia cētera terram,
ōs hominī sublīme dedit caelumque tuērī jussit et
ērēctōs ad sīdera tollere vultūs.

Although other animals look at the ground facing downward *(Prōna)*
[Prometheus] gave an uplifted face to man, and ordered him to gaze at
the heavens and to lift his face upright to the stars.

(Ovid, Metamorphoses 1.84–6)

989

Caveat ēmptor!

Let the buyer beware.

(Legal)

990

Duplex fit bonitās, simul accessit celeritās.

A benefit becomes double as soon as swiftness is added.

(Publilius Syrus, Sententia 141)

991

Quī vincī sēsē patitur prō tempore, vincit.

Who allows himself to be conquered according to circumstances, wins.

(Dionysius Cato)

992

Paucōrum est intellegere quid dōnet Deus.

It is given to few people to know what God gives.

(*Publilius Syrus*, Sententia 480, *adapted*)

993

Sequitur vēr hiemem.

Spring follows winter.

(*Anonymous*)

994

Nōn prōgredī est regredī.

Not to advance is to go backward.

(*Motto*)

995

Placeat hominī quidquid Deō placuit.

What is pleasing to God should be pleasing to man.

(*Seneca*, Epistulae Morales 74.20)

996

Interdum stultus bene loquitur.

Sometimes a foolish man speaks well.

(*Anonymous*)

997

Habeās corpus.
You may have the body.
(Legal)

998

Sex hōrīs dormīre sat est juvenīque senīque:
septem vix pigrō, nūllī concēdimus octō.
To sleep six hours is enough for young and old;
with difficulty we grant seven hours to the lazy, but eight hours to no one.
(Medieval)

999

In silvam nōn ligna ferās.
You should not carry wood into the forest.
(Horace, Satires 1.10.34)

1000

Quōcumque aspexī, nihil est nisi mortis imāgo.
Wherever I look, there is nothing except the image of death.
(Ovid, Tristia 1.11.23)

1001
Ut flammam minuās, ligna focō retrahās.
In order to lessen the flame, you should remove the wood from the fireplace.
(Medieval)

1002
Nōmina stultōrum scrībuntur ubīque locōrum.
Names of stupid people are written everywhere [ubīque locōrum].
(Medieval)

1003
Quī loquitur quod vult, quod nōn vult audiet ille;
quīque facit quod vult, quod nōn vult sufferet ille.
He who says what he wants will hear what he does not want; and he who
does what he wants will endure what he does not want.
(Medieval)

1004

Aulae vānitātem, Forī ambitiōnem rīdēre mēcum soleō.

I am accustomed to laugh to myself at the vanity of the court
and the ambition of the Forum.
(Medieval)

1005

Scīre loquī decus est; decus est et scīre tacēre.

It is a virtue to know how to speak;
it is also a virtue to know how to be silent.
(Anonymous)

1006

Tacēre quī nescit, nescit et loquī.

He who does not know how to be silent does not even know how to speak.
(Anonymous)

1007

Pessima sit, nūllī nōn sua forma placet.

[Although] she may be terribly ugly, her own appearance pleases every girl.
(Ovid, Ars Amatoria 1.614)

1008

Quid nōn possit amor?

What can love not accomplish?
(Anonymous)

1009
Fortūnam citius reperiās quam retineās.
You can more quickly find good fortune than keep it.
(*Publilius Syrus*, Sententia 168)

1010
Mōbilior ventīs...fēmina.
Woman is more fickle than the wind.
(*Calpurnius*, Eclogues 3.10)

1011
Quid magis est dūrum saxō? Quid mollius undā?
Dūra tamen mollī saxa cavantur aquā.
What is harder than rock? What is softer than water? Yet hard rocks are
carved out by soft water.
(*Ovid*, Ars Amatoria 1.475–6)

1012
Saepius opīniōne quam rē labōrāmus.
We are more often troubled by our thoughts about a matter
than by the matter itself.
(*Seneca*, Epistulae Morales 13.4)

1013
Melior est canis vīvus leōne mortuō.
A live dog is better than a dead lion.
(Ecclesiastes 9.4 *[St. Jerome's Vulgate translation]*)

1014
Melior tūtiorque est certa pāx quam spērāta victōria; haec in tuā, illa in deōrum manū est.
Sure peace is better and safer than hoped-for victory;
the former lies in your hands, the latter in the hands of the gods.
(*Livy*, Ab Urbe Condita 30.30)

1015
Nēmō ita pauper vīvit quam pauper nātus est.
No one lives as poor as he was born.
(*Anonymous*)

1016

Parēns īrātus in sē est crūdēlissimus.

The angry parent is most cruel towards himself.
(*Publilius Syrus*, Sententia 466)

1017

Nīl habet īnfēlīx paupertās dūrius in sē quam quod rīdiculōs hominēs facit.

Wretched poverty has nothing harsher in it
than the fact that it makes men ridiculous.
(*Juvenal*, Satires 3.152–153)

1018

In silvam nōn ligna ferās īnsānius.

You could not more insanely carry wood into the forest
[than to do what you are trying to do now].
(*Horace*, Satires 1.10.34)

1019

Quid levius ventō? Fulmen. Quid fulmine? Fāma. Quis fāmā? Mulier. Quid muliere? Nihil.

What is more fickle than the wind? A thunderbolt. What more fickle than the
thunderbolt? Reputation. What more fickle than reputation? Woman.
What more fickle than woman? Nothing.
(*Medieval*)

1020

Errāre mālō cum Platōne quam cum istīs vēra sentīre.

I prefer to be wrong with Plato than to know the truth with those people.

(*M. Tullius Cicero*, Tusculanae Disputationes 1.17.39, *adapted*)

1021

Hominēs amplius oculīs quam auribus crēdunt:
longum iter est per praecepta,
breve et efficāx per exempla.

Men believe their eyes rather than their ears; it is a long journey through advice, but a short and easy one through examples.

(*Seneca*, Epistulae Morales 6.5)

1022

Hoc est melle dulcī dulcius.

This is more delicious than delicious honey.

(*Plautus*, Truculentus 371)

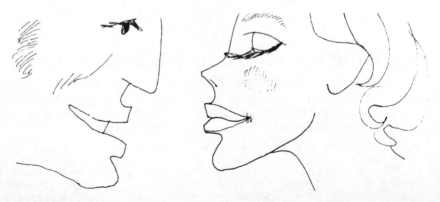

1023
Nihil est...vēritātis lūce dulcius.
Nothing is more pleasant than the light of truth.
(*M. Tullius Cicero*, Academicae Quaestiones 2.10.31, *adapted*)

1024
Plūrēs amīcōs mēnsa quam mēns concipit.
A person's table attracts more friends than his mind.
(*Publilius Syrus*, Sententia 670)

1025
Nihil est tam volucre quam male dictum, nihil facilius ēmittitur, nihil citius excipitur, nihil lātius dissipātur.
Nothing is so swift as gossip, nothing is more easily let go, nothing is more quickly picked up, nothing is more widely scattered.
(*M. Tullius Cicero*, Pro Plancio 23.57)

1026
Nōn ōvum tam simile ōvō.
An egg is not so like an egg [as this person is like that person].
(*Quintilian*, 5.11.30)

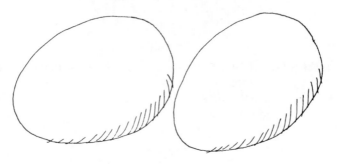

1027
Graviōra quaedam sunt remedia perīculīs.
Certain remedies are more dangerous than the perils [they may prevent].
(*Anonymous*)

1028
Fidēliōrēs sunt oculī auribus.
Eyes are more trustworthy than ears.
(*Medieval*)

1029
Dum loquor, hōra fugit.
While I am talking, time is flying.
(*Ovid*, Amores 1.11.15)

1030

Discere sī quaeris, doceās! Sīc ipse docēris.

If you wish to learn, teach. Thus you yourself are instructed.
(Medieval)

1031

Nunc populus est domī leōnēs, forīs vulpēs.

Now the people are lions at home, foxes out of doors.
(*Petronius,* Satyricon 44.4)

1032

Orimur, morimur.

We rise (are born) and we die.
(Anonymous)

1033

Dum loquimur, fūgerit invida aetās.

While we are talking, envious time will have passed by.
(*Horace,* Odes 1.11.7–8)

1034

**Cum essem parvulus, loquēbar ut parvulus,
sapiēbam ut parvulus, cōgitābam ut parvulus.**

When I was a child, I spoke as a child, I reasoned as a child, I thought as a child.
(*Paul,* I Corinthians 13.11 [*St. Jerome's Vulgate translation*])

1035

Vīvāmus ergō mōribus praeteritis; praesentibus verbīs loquāmur.

Therefore let us live by ancient morals; but let us speak with words of today.
(*Macrobius*, Saturnalia 1.5.2)

1036

Magnōs hominēs virtūte mētīmur, nōn fortūnā.

We measure great men by their courage, not by their luck.
(*Cornelius Nepos*, Eumenes 1.1)

1037

Nāscimur in lacrimīs, lacrimābile dūcimus aevum; clauditur in lacrimīs ultima nostra diēs.

We are born in tears, we lead a tearful life; our last day closes in tears.
(*Anonymous*)

1038

In quō... jūdiciō jūdicāveritis, jūdicābiminī.

In what judgment you judge, you shall be judged.
(Matthew 7.2 *[St. Jerome's Vulgate translation]*)

1039

Inter majōrēs caveās nē multa loquāris.

Take care not to speak too much in the presence of more powerful people.

(Medieval)

1040

Tot mala sum passus quot in aethere sīdera lūcent.

I have suffered as many evils as there are stars shining in the sky.

(Ovid, Tristia 1.5.47)

1041

Omne sub rēgnō graviōre rēgnum.

Every power is under a stronger power.

(Medieval)

1042

Quōs Deus vult perdere prius dēmentat.

Whom God wishes to destroy he first makes mad.

(Fragment of Euripides, said to have been translated by Barnes)

1043

**Egō deum genus esse semper dīxī et dīcam caelitum:
sed eōs nōn cūrāre opīnor quid agat hūmānum genus.
Nam sī cūrent, bene bonīs sit, male malīs.
Quod nunc abest.**

I have always said and will say that the heavenly race of gods exists;
but I believe that they do not care what the human race does.
For if they did care, it would go well for the good people and poorly
for the bad people, but this is far from existing.
(*Ennius*, Fragments 208–9)

1044

Lacrimāns nātus sum et lacrimāns morior.

I was born weeping, and I die weeping.
(*Medieval*)

1045

Tuēbor.

I shall defend.
(*Motto of the State of Michigan*)

1046

Nōn tam aqua similis aquae.

A drop of water is not so like another drop of water [as this person is like
another person].
(*Plautus*, Menaechmi 1089, *adapted*)

1047
Rōmae quoque hominēs moriuntur.
Men also die at Rome.
(Medieval)

1048
Nōn inultus premor.
I am not injured unavenged.
(Motto of Nancy, France)

1049
Medice, cūrā tē ipsum.
Physician, heal thyself.
(Luke 4.23 *[St. Jerome's Vulgate translation]*)

1050
Sī vīs pācem, parā bellum.
If you wish peace, prepare for war.
(Anonymous)

1051
**Nōn nōbīs, Domine, nōn nōbīs,
sed nōminī tuō dā glōriam.**
Give glory, not to us, O Lord, not to us, but to thy name.
(Anonymous)

1052

**Crēde mihī, bene quī latuit bene vīxit,
et intrā fortūnam dēbet quisque manēre suam.**

Believe me, the person has led a good life who has kept well concealed;
and each person should stay within the limits of his fortune.
(*Ovid*, Tristia 3.4.25–26)

1053

Sī monumentum requīris, circumspice.

If you seek [his] monument, look around you.
(*Inscription in St. Paul's Cathedral, London,
concerning its architect, Sir Christopher Wren, 1632–1723*)

1054

Sī quiētem māvīs, dūc uxōrem parem.

If you prefer quiet, marry a wife equal [to your own station in life].
(*Quintilian*, Declamationes Maiores 257.47)

1055

Mūnera, crēde mihī, capiunt hominēsque deōsque.

Believe me, gifts capture both gods and men.
(*Ovid*, Ars Amatoria 3.653)

1056

Nōsce tē ipsum.

Know thyself.

(Translation of saying of the oracle at Delphi)

1057

Disce aut discēde.

Learn or get out.

(Common school motto)

1058

Rem tenē, verba sequentur.

Hold to your subject; the words will follow.

(Cato in Gaius Julius Victor, Ars Rhetorica 1, *fourth century AD)*

1059

Vāde ad formīcam, Ō piger, et cōnsīderā viās ejus et disce sapientiam.

Go to the ant, O lazy one, and consider its ways and learn wisdom.

(Proverbs 6.6 [St. Jerome's Vulgate translation])

1060

Adde parvum parvō; magnus acervus erit.

Add a little to a little; there will be a large heap.

(Anonymous)

1061
Vīve ut vīvās.
Live in order to live [happily].
(Motto)

1062
Sī vīs amārī, amā.
If you wish to be loved, give love.
(Anonymous)

1063
Redde Caesarī quae sunt Caesaris et quae sunt Deī, Deō.
Give to Caesar those things which are Caesar's
and to God the things which are God's.
(Attributed to Jesus in Matthew 22.21 *[St. Jerome's Vulgate translation])*

1064
Dā locum melioribus.
Give your place to your betters.
(Terence, Phormio 522)

1065
Sperne lucrum; versat mentēs īnsāna cupīdō.
Avoid gain: mad desire turns men's minds.
(Sayings of the Twelve Wise Men, Poetae Latini Minores 4, p. 199)

1066
Crēde mihī, miserōs prūdentia prīma relinquit.
Believe me, caution is the first thing that leaves unhappy people.
(*Ovid*, Epistulae Ex Ponto 4.12.47)

1067
Dā dextram miserō.
Give your right hand (helping hand) to an unfortunate.
(*Vergil*, Aeneid 6.370)

1068
Deum cole, rēgem servā.
Worship God, guard the King.
(*Motto*)

1069
Flērēs sī scīrēs ūnum tua tempora mēnsem; rīdēs cum nōn sit forsitan ūna diēs.
You would weep if you knew that your time was a single month;
you laugh when it is perhaps not a single day.
(*Anonymous*)

1070
Deō duce, Fortūnā comitante.
With God as our leader, and with Fortune accompanying us.
(*Motto*)

1071

Sērius aut citius sēdem properāmus ad ūnam.

Sooner or later we hasten to the same home.

(*Ovid*, Metamorphoses 10.33)

1072

**Ut nōn multa loquī, plūra autem audīre monēret,
linguam ūnam nātūra, duās dedit omnibus aurēs.**

To advise us to speak little, but to hear much; nature has given us all one
mouth, but two ears.

(*Marcus Muretus*, 1526–1585)

1073

**Absurdum est ut aliōs regat,
quī sē ipsum regere nescit.**

It is ridiculous that a person who does not know how to rule himself
should rule others.

(*Anonymous*)

1074

**Crēvērunt et opēs et opum furiāta cupīdō;
et cum possideant plūrima, plūra volunt.**

Both wealth and the mad desire for wealth have increased;
and when they [finally] possess a great deal, they want more.

(*Ovid*, Fasti 1.211–2)

1075

Inventa sunt specula ut homō ipse sē nōsset.

Mirrors were invented so that a man might know himself.
(*Seneca*, Naturales Quaestiones 1.17.4)

1076

Nītimur in vetitum semper, cupimusque negāta.

We always strive toward forbidden things and we wish for those things which are denied.
(*Ovid*, Amores 3.4.17)

1077

Aure lupī vīsā, sequitur certissima cauda.

When the wolf's ear is seen, his tail will most certainly follow.
(*Medieval*)

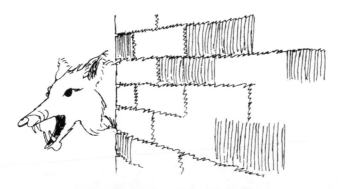

1078

Amor et lacrima oculīs oritur, in pectus cadit.

Love and tears spring from the eyes and fall into the heart.
(*Publilius Syrus,* Sententia 40)

1079

Turpe est ōdisse quem laudēs.

It is disgraceful to have hated the person whom you should praise.
(*Anonymous*)

1080

Multa quidem scrīpsī; sed quae vitiōsa putāvī ēmendātūrīs ignibus ipse dedī.

Indeed I have written a great deal; but those things which I thought faulty
I myself have given to the fires that would correct them.
(*Ovid,* Tristia 4.10.61–2)

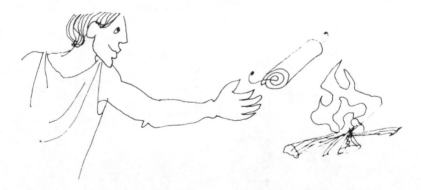

1081

**Nihil turpius quam grandis nātū senex,
quī nūllum aliud habet argūmentum,
quō sē probet diū vīxisse, praeter aetātem.**

There is nothing more disgraceful than an old man advanced in years
who has no other argument by which he may prove that he has lived
a long time except his age.

(*Seneca*, De Tranquillitate 3.8, *adapted*)

1082

**Adhūc nēminem cognōvī poētam... quī sibī
nōn optimus vidērētur.**

Up to now I have known no poet ... who did not seem to himself
to be the best.

(*M. Tullius Cicero*, Tusculanae Disputationes 5.22.63)

1083

Sānctissimum est meminisse cui tē dēbeās.

It is most sacred [of all things] to have remembered to whom you are indebted.

(*Publilius Syrus*, Sententia 588)

1084

Nūlla tam bona est fortūna dē quā nihil possīs querī.

No fortune is so good that you cannot make some complaint about it.

(*Publilius Syrus*, Sententia 384)

1085

Optimum est patī quod ēmendāre nōn possīs.

It is best to endure what you cannot correct.

(*Seneca,* Epistulae Morales 107.9)

1086

Mortālis nēmō est quem nōn attingat dolor morbusve.

There is no mortal whom pain and disease do not touch.

(*M. Tullius Cicero,* Tusculanae Disputationes 3.25.59 [*translation of* Euripides])

1087

Quae fuit dūrum patī, meminisse dulce est.

It is sweet to have remembered what was difficult to endure.

(*Seneca,* Hercules Furens 656–57)

1088

Nūllum est jam dictum quod nōn dictum sit prius.

There is nothing said now which has not been said before.

(*Terence,* Eunuchus 41)

1089

Date et dabitur vōbīs.

Give and it will be given unto you.

(Luke 6.38 [*St. Jerome's Vulgate translation*])

1090

Gubernāculum quod alterī nāvī magnum, alterī exiguum est.

A rudder which is large for one ship is small for another.
(*Seneca,* Epistulae Morales 43.2)

1091

Nēmō errat ūnī sibī, sed dēmentiam spargit in proximōs accipitque in vicem.

No one is wrong to himself alone, but he spreads his madness toward those
who are near him and receives it in return.
(*Seneca,* Epistulae Morales 94.54)

1092

Infirmōs cūrāte, mortuōs suscitāte, leprōsōs mundāte, daemonēs ējicite: grātīs accēpistis, grātīs date.

Cure the sick, raise the dead, cleanse the lepers, cast out demons: you have
freely received; freely give.
(Matthew 10.8 *[St. Jerome's Vulgate translation]*)

1093

Secundīs nēmō cōnfīdat; adversīs nēmō dēficiat; alternae sunt vicēs rērum.

Let no one trust in favorable [circumstances]; and let no one fail in adverse
[circumstances]; [for] circumstances [always] change.
(*Seneca,* Naturales Quaestiones 3, praefatio 7)

1094

Quis enim virtūtem amplectitur
ipsam praemia sī tollās?

For who embraces virtue for itself if you should remove the rewards?

(Medieval)

1095

Ab aliō exspectēs alterī quod fēcerīs.

You should expect from one person what you have done to another.

(Publilius Syrus, Sententia 2)

1096

Quod tibī fīerī nōn vīs, alterī nē fēcerīs.

You should not do to someone else what you do not want done to yourself.

(Lampridius, Alexander Severus 51.6, *adapted)*

1097

Flūmina pauca vidēs dē magnīs fontibus orta.

You see few rivers that rise from large springs.

(Ovid, Remedia Amoris 97)

1098

Inde lupī spērēs caudam, cum vīderis aurēs.

When you have seen the ears, then you may hope for the tail of the wolf.

(Medieval)

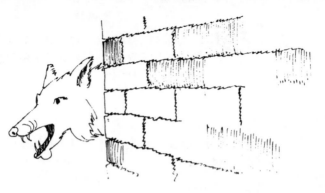

1099

Ōderint, dum metuant.

Let them hate [me] provided they fear [me].

(Accius, Atreus fragment 168)

1100

Ō praeclārum custōdem ovium, ut ajunt, lupum!

As they say, O wonderful guardian of the sheep, a wolf!

(M. Tullius Cicero, Philippics 3.11.27)

1101

Quamvīs per multōs cuculus cantāverit annōs, dīcere nescit adhūc aliud verbum nisi "Cuccūc."

Although the cuckoo has sung for many years, he still doesn't know how to say any word except "cuckoo."

(Medieval)

235

1102
Mālō quam bene olēre nīl olēre.
I prefer not to smell at all than to smell good.
(*Martial*, 6.55.5)

1103
Proprium hūmānī ingeniī est ōdisse quem laeserīs.
It is characteristic of human nature to hate the person whom you have harmed.
(*Tacitus*, Agricola 42)

1104
Mora omnis odiō est, sed facit sapientiam.
Every delay is hateful, but it creates wisdom.
(*Publilius Syrus*, Sententia 311)

1105
Stultōrum plēna sunt omnia.
All [places] are full of stupid people.
(*M. Tullius Cicero*, Ad Familiares 9.22)

1106
Quoniam nōn potest id fīerī quod vīs,
id velīs quod possit.
Because what you want cannot happen, you should wish for that which can.
(*Terence*, Andria 305–6)

1107
Optimum est aliēnā fruī experientiā.

It is best to profit by someone else's experience.

(Anonymous)

1108
Quī caret argentō, frūstrā ūtitur argūmentō.

He who lacks silver uses argument in vain.

(Anonymous)

1109
Brevēs haustūs in philosophiā ad atheismum dūcunt, lārgiōrēs autem redūcunt ad Deum.

In philosophy, short sips lead to atheism, but more ample ones bring a person back to God.

(Sir Francis Bacon, 1561–1626, of Atheism)

1110
Vītaque mancipiō nūllī datur, omnibus ūsū.

Life is given to no one as a possession, (but it is given) to everyone to use.

(Lucretius, De Rerum Natura 3.971)

1111

**Parvula — nam exemplō est — magnī formīca labōris
ōre trahit quodcumque potest atque addit acervō
quem struit, haud īgnāra ac nōn incauta futūrī.**

For this will serve as an example: the small ant of great [capacity for] work
drags with her mouth whatever she can and adds it to the pile which she is
building, not at all unknowing or careless about the future.

(*Horace*, Satires 1.1.33–35)

1112

**Nōlīte thēsaurizāre vōbīs thēsaurōs in terrā....
Thēsaurizāte autem vōbīs thēsaurōs in caelō.**

Do not set up treasures for yourselves on earth,
but rather set up treasures for yourselves in heaven.

(Matthew 6.19–20 *[St. Jerome's Vulgate translation]*)

1113

Plūrēs crāpula quam gladius.

Drunkenness [has killed] more (people) than the sword.

(*Anonymous*)

1114

Pūblicum bonum prīvātō est praeferendum.

The public good must be preferred to private.

(*Legal*)

1115

Oculīs magis habenda fidēs quam auribus.

More faith should be given to the eyes than to the ears.

(*Anonymous*)

1116

Aliēnō mōre vīvendum est mihī.

I have to live by somebody else's rules.

(*Terence*, Andria 152)

1117

Et post malam segetem serendum est.

One must sow [again] even after a bad crop.

(*Seneca*, Epistulae Morales 81.1)

1118

Etiam senī est discendum.

Even an old man must learn.

(*Seneca*, Epistulae Morales 76.3)

1119

Omnia hominī dum vīvit spēranda sunt.

Man must hope for all things as long as he is alive.

(*Seneca*, Epistulae Morales 70.6)

1120
Ūtendum est dīvitiīs, nōn abūtendum.
Riches should be used, not abused.
(Anonymous)

1121
Mūsīs et amīcīs omnī tempore serviendum amōre, mōre, ōre, rē.
We should serve the Muses and our friends at all times
with love, manners, conversation, and material assistance.
(Medieval)

1122
Mīranda canunt sed nōn crēdenda poētae.
The poets sing things which should be admired but not believed.
(Dionysius Cato, 3.18)

1123
Virtūs...cōnstat ex hominibus tuendīs.
Virtue...consists of protecting mankind.
(M. Tullius Cicero, De Officiis 1.44.157)

1124
Plūrēs occīdit gula quam gladius.
The throat has killed more than the sword.
(Anonymous)

1125

Multa īgnōscendō fit potēns potentior.

By pardoning many things, the powerful man becomes more powerful.
(*Publilius Syrus*, Sententia 350)

1126

Ēripuitque Jovī fulmen vīrēsque tonandī.

It (philosophy) seized from Jupiter
the thunderbolt and the strength of his thundering.
(*Manilius*, 1.104)

1127

Hī nōn vīdērunt, ut ad cursum equum, ad arandum bovem, ad indāgandum canem, sīc hominem ad duās rēs (ut ait Aristotelēs) ad intellegendum et ad agendum esse nātum.

They have not seen that as a horse is born for running, a bull for plowing,
a dog for tracking, so a man, as Aristotle says, is born for two things:
for understanding and for acting.
(*M. Tullius Cicero*, De Finibus 2.13.40)

1128

Cēde repūgnantī: cēdendō victor abībis.

Yield to the one who fights back; by yielding you will go away a victor.
(*Ovid*, Ars Amatoria 2.197)

1129

Gutta cavat lapidem nōn vī sed saepe cadendō.

The drop (of water) carves the stone not by force, but by frequently falling.
(Medieval)

1130

Nihil est tam incrēdibile quod nōn dīcendō fīat probābile; nihil tam horridum, tam incultum quod nōn splendēscat ōrātiōne et tamquam excolātur.

Nothing is so unbelievable that it cannot become probable by speaking; nothing is so crude [and] so uncouth that it may not shine by eloquence and, as it were, be improved.
(M. Tullius Cicero, Paradoxa Stoicorum 3)

1131

Nimium altercandō vēritās āmittitur.

Truth is lost by too much argumentation.
(Publilius Syrus, Sententia 416)

1132

Dīvitiae apud sapientem virum in servitūte sunt, apud stultum in imperiō.

For a wise man, riches are in bondage; for a stupid man, they are in command.
(Seneca, De Vita Beata 26.1)

1133

Alitur vitium crēscitque tegendō.

Vice is fed and grows by concealment.
*(Robert Burton, 1577–1640, English writer
and author of* The Anatomy of Melancholy*)*

1134

Quō modō fābula, sīc vīta: nōn quam diū sed quam bene ācta sit rēfert.

As a play is, so is life; it does not matter how long it is acted, but how well.
(Seneca, Epistulae Morales 77.20)

1135

Mendācem memorem esse oportet.

It is necessary that a liar have a good memory.
(Quintilian, Institutio Oratoria 4.2.91)

1136

Quae...domus tam stabilis, quae tam firma cīvitās est quae nōn discidiīs funditus possit ēvertī?

What home is so stable, what state is so firm, which cannot be overturned
from its foundations by dissension?
(M. Tullius Cicero, De Amicitia 7.23)

1137

Ūnus homō nōbīs cūnctandō restituit rem.

One man by waiting restored the state to us.
(*Ennius,* Annales Fragment 286)

1138

**Cārī sunt parentēs, cārī līberī, propinquī, familiārēs,
sed omnēs omnium cāritātēs patria ūna complexa est:
prō quā quis bonus dubitet mortem oppetere,
sī eī sit prōfutūrus?**

Parents are dear, children are dear, relatives, friends; but our fatherland alone
embraces all the affections of everyone. What honest man would hesitate to
meet death for his country if he would benefit it?
(*M. Tullius Cicero,* De Officiis 1.17.57)

1139

Id dictū quam rē facilius est.

This is easier to say than to do.
(*Livy,* Ab Urbe Condita 31.38)

1140

Est captū facilis turbātā piscis in undā.

A fish is easy to capture in troubled waters.
(*Medieval*)

1141

Et sīc dēmōnstrātur quod erat dēmōnstrandum.

And thus is shown what was to be shown.

(Anonymous)

1142

**Hās tantās virtūtēs ingentia vitia aequābant:
inhūmāna crūdēlitās, perfidia plūs quam Pūnica,
nihil vērī, nihil sānctī, nūllus deōrum metus,
nūllum jūs jūrandum, nūlla religiō.**

Enormous vices equaled these great virtues: inhuman cruelty, treachery
greater than Carthaginian, no sense of truth, no sense of what is sacred,
no fear of the gods, no respect for an oath, no sense of religion.

(Livy, Ab Urbe Condita 21.4)

1143

**Nihil tam difficile est
quīn quaerendō investīgārī possit.**

Nothing is so difficult but that it can be investigated by searching.

(Terence, Heauton Timoroumenos 675)

1144

Forsan et haec ōlim meminisse juvābit.

Perhaps some day it will be pleasing [to you] to remember these things.

(Vergil, Aeneid 1.203)

1145

Dum modo sit dīves, barbarus ipse placet.

Provided he is rich, the barbarian himself is pleasing.
(*Ovid*, Ars Amatoria 2.276)

1146

Nōn licet omnibus adīre Corinthum.

It is not permitted to everyone to go to Corinth.
(*Anonymous*)

1147

Ultima semper exspectanda diēs hominī est, dīcīque beātus ante obitum nēmō suprēmaque fūnera dēbet.

The last day must always be awaited by man, and no one should be called
happy before his death and the last rites.
(*Ovid*, Metamorphoses 3.135–7)

1148

Jūcundissima nāvigātiō juxtā terram; ambulātiō juxtā mare.

Navigation is most pleasant near the land, and walking, near the sea.
(*Anonymous*)

1149

Optimum est patī quod ēmendāre nōn possīs.

It is best to endure what you cannot correct.

(*Anonymous*)

1150

**Quid prōdest forīs esse strēnuum,
sī domī male vīvitur?**

What good is it to be energetic outside of the house
if your life at home is bad?

(*Valerius Maximus*, Facta et Dicta Memorabilia 2.9.1)

1151

Laus nova nisi oritur, etiam vetus āmittitur.

Unless new praise arises, even the old praise is lost.

(*Publilius Syrus*, Sententia 293)

1152

Decet verēcundum esse adulēscentem.

It is fitting for a young man to be modest.

(*Plautus*, Asinaria 833)

1153

Altissima quaeque flūmina minimō sonō lābuntur.

And the deepest rivers flow with the least sound.

(*Q. Curtius Rufus*, 7.4.13)

1154

Stultitia est vēnātum dūcere invītās canēs.

It is stupidity to take unwilling dogs to hunt.
(*Plautus*, Stichus 139)

1155

Nūlla causa jūsta cuiquam esse potest contrā patriam arma capiendī.

There can be no just reason for anyone to take up arms against his country.
(*M. Tullius Cicero*, Philippics 2.22.53)

1156

Neque habet plūs sapientiae quam lapis.

He has no more wisdom than a stone.
(*Plautus*, Miles Gloriosus 236)

1157

Nūlla tempestās magna perdūrat; procellae quantō plūs habent vīrium, tantō minus temporis.

No great storm lasts;
the more strength the winds have, so much shorter is the time.
(*Seneca*, Naturales Quaestiones 7.9.3)

1158

Nūlla possessiō, nūlla vīs aurī et argentī plūris quam virtūs aestimanda.

No possession, no wealth of gold and silver should be considered of more value than virtue.

(*M. Tullius Cicero*, Paradoxa Stoicorum 6.48)

1159

**Nēmō est tam senex
quī sē annum nōn putet posse vīvere.**

No one is so old that he does not believe that he can live a year [longer].

(*M. Tullius Cicero*, De Senectute 7.24)

1160

Septem hōrās dormīsse sat est juvenīque senīque.

To have slept for seven hours is enough for young and old.

(*Medieval*)

1161

Viam quī nescit quā dēveniat ad mare, eum oportet amnem quaerere comitem sibī.

He who does not know the way by which he may come to the sea ought to look for a stream as a companion for himself.

(*Plautus*, Poenulus 627–8)

1162
Rāra avis in terrīs nigrōque simillima cycnō.
A rare bird on earth and most like a black swan.
(*Juvenal*, Satires 6.165)

1163
Nōn aquā, nōn ignī ut ajunt,
locīs plūribus ūtimur quam amīcitiā.
We do not use water or fire, as they say,
in more places than we use friendship.
(*M. Tullius Cicero*, De Amicitia 6.22)

1164
Suae quemque fortūnae maximē paenitet..
Each one regrets his own fortune most of all.
(*M. Tullius Cicero*, Ad Familiares 6.1)

1165
Scelere vēlandum est scelus.
Crime must be hidden by [further] crime.
(*Seneca*, Phaedra 721)

1166

Nōn rēfert quam multōs librōs
sed quam bonōs habeās.

It does not matter how many books you have, but how good [they are].
(Anonymous)

1167

Scientia quae est remōta ā jūstitiā calliditās potius
quam sapientia est appellanda.

Knowledge which is removed from justice
should be called shrewdness rather than wisdom.
(M. Tullius Cicero, De Officiis 1.19.63)

1168

Nōn dēs rēs cūnctās quae optat avāra voluptās:
nōn catulō dētur, quotiēns sua cauda movētur.

You should not give everything which greedy pleasure wants;
a puppy should not be given things as often as he moves his tail.
(Medieval)

1169

Suum quisque nōscat ingenium, ācremque sē et
bonōrum et vitiōrum suōrum jūdicem praebeat.

Each one should know his own nature and should make himself be a keen
judge both of his virtues and his faults.
(M. Tullius Cicero, De Officiis 1.31.114)

1170
Sequitur superbōs ultor ā tergō deus.
An avenging god follows the haughty [closely] from the rear.
(*Seneca*, Hercules Furens 385)

1171
Firmissima est inter parēs amīcitia.
Friendship is firmest among equals.
(*Q. Curtius Rufus*, 7.8.27)

1172
In cane sagācitās prīma est sī investīgāre dēbet ferās, cursus sī cōnsequī, audācia sī mordēre et invādere.
In a dog, keenness of scent is the first thing if he is supposed to track animals; swiftness, if he is supposed to overtake them; boldness, if he is supposed to bite and attack them.
(*Seneca*, Epistulae Morales 76.8)

1173
Vīnum etiam senēs addūcit ut saltent vel nōlentēs.
Wine leads even old men to dance, even when they are unwilling.
(*Translation of Eriphus*)

1174

Cōnsequitur quodcumque petit.

He gets whatever he seeks.
(Motto)

1175

Quodcumque libuit facere victōrī, licet.

The victor is permitted to do whatever he wants.
(Seneca, De Tranquillitate 335)

1176

Crētizandum est cum Crēte.

One should act like a Cretan with a Cretan.
(Anonymous)

1177

Trīste... est nōmen ipsum carendī.

The very name of "want" is sad.
(M. Tullius Cicero, Tusculanae Disputationes 1.36.87)

1178

Longius aut propius mors sua quemque manet.

Sooner or later his own death remains for each person.
(Propertius, 2.28.58)

1179
Fatētur facinus is quī jūdicium fugit.
He who flees from judgment confesses his crime.
(*Publilius Syrus,* Sententia 174)

1180
Exīstimō in summō imperātōre quattuor hās rēs inesse oportēre: scientiam reī mīlitāris, virtūtem, auctōritātem, fēlīcitātem.
I think that in the supreme commander there should be these four things:
a knowledge of military science, courage, authority [and] good fortune.
(*M. Tullius Cicero,* Pro Lege Manilia 10.28)

1181
Cantābit vacuus cōram latrōne viātor.
The traveler who has nothing will sing in the presence of a highwayman.
(*Juvenal,* Satires 10.22)

1182
Tempora lābuntur mōre fluentis aquae.
Times slip by in the manner of flowing water.
(*Motto on a sundial*)

1183

Sed quō Fāta trahunt, virtūs sēcūra sequētur.

But virtue will safely follow wherever the Fates lead.

(*Lucan*, Pharsalia 2.287)

1184

Ūtendum est aetāte: citō pede lābitur aetās.

Life should be used; for life slips by on rapid feet.

(*Ovid*, Ars Amatoria 3.65)

1185

**Aedificāre in tuō propriō
solō nōn licet quod alterī noceat.**

It is not permitted to build on your own soil that which may harm another.

(*Legal*)

1186

Tempus erit, quō vōs speculum vīdisse pigēbit.

The time will come when it will displease you to have seen your mirror.

(*Ovid*, Medicamina Faciei 47)

1187

Oportet ferrum tundere, dum rubet.

It is necessary to strike the iron while it glows.

(*Anonymous*)

Rēbus in hūmānīs tria sunt dīgnissima laude: uxor casta, bonus socius, sincērus amīcus.

In human affairs, there are three things most worthy of praise: a loyal wife, a good ally, and a sincere friend.

(Medieval)

Topical Index

F

G

H

I

R

rabbit, *416, 453*
rashness, *435, 896*
Rathskeller, *962*
read/reading, *58, 364, 678*
reap, *447*
reason (*ratio*), *105, 278, 554, 597, 656, 799, 808, 949, 1155*
refuse, *420*
regret, *1164*
rejoice, *126, 180*
relatives, *1138*
religion, *167, 1142*
remedy, *490, 588, 611, 626, 1027*
remember, *677, 1144*
repetition, *593*
reputation, *45, 527, 674, 979, 1019*
respect, *1142*
result, *147*
reward, *583, 865, 897, 899, 1094*
rhetorician, *874*
rich/wealthy, *947, 1145*
riches/wealth, *209, 213, 482, 527, 693, 701, 747, 1120, 1132*
ridiculous, *1017, 1073*
ring, *357*
rivalry, *41*
river, *234, 310, 508, 535, 672, 687, 768, 911, 977, 1097, 1153*
robber/thief, *18, 23, 489, 1181*
rock, *1011*
Roman people, *731, 938*
Rome, *27, 244, 538, 562, 591, 765, 907, 1047*
rose, *413, 805*
rudder, *1090*
rule (verb) *24, 42, 60, 92, 267, 395, 880, 965, 1073*
rule/guide, *78, 271*
rule/law, *175, 1116*
rule/power, *388, 1041*
ruler, *212, 750*

S

sadness, *566, 653, 948, 1177*
safety, *115, 135, 145, 257, 340, 429, 556, 618, 885, 1014, 1183*
sailor, *851*
salt, *892, 980*
salvation, *81*
scepter, *764*
science, *254*
scorn, *842*
scorpion, *575, 841*
sea, *284, 1149, 1161*
seashell, *878*
secret, *282*
security, *15*
senate, *11*
sense, *639*
senses, *704*
servitude, *209*
shadow, *36, 903*
sheep, *165, 228, 238, 470, 851, 1100*
shepherd, *228, 851*
shield, *400*
ship, *326, 409, 966, 1090*
shipwreck, *189, 408, 506, 531, 589*
sick man, *411, 626, 661, 689, 697, 819, 930, 1092*
silent/quiet, *232, 275, 299, 316, 459, 546, 665, 680, 696, 950, 970, 1005, 1006, 1153*
silver, *1108, 1158*
sin, *871, 894, 985*
sing, *1101, 1122, 1181*
sister, *547*
skin, *236*
slave/servant, *97, 212, 437, 540, 783*
slavery, *217, 491, 938*
sleep, *551, 631, 910, 998, 1160*
slowness, *683*
smell/scent, *427, 638, 1102, 1172*
smoke, *114, 373, 505, 790*
snail, *683*
snake, *67*

Author Index

Classical Latin Authors and the Titles of their Works Quoted in Latin Proverbs

(references are to quotation numbers)

Note: Where content is not evident from the title of a work, a very brief description is offered for the convenience of the reader.

Accius [Lucius Accius] (170–86 BC), Roman tragic playwright
Atreus (a tragedy) *1099*

Ammianus Marcellinus (ca. AD 330–395), Roman historian, born at Antioch
A History of Rome from the Reign of Nerva (AD 96–378) *114*

Annaeus Seneca, see **Seneca**

Apuleius [Lucius Apuleius] (ca. AD 125–ca. 170), philosopher, born in Africa Proconsularis
Metamorphoses (also known as *The Golden Ass*: A novel about a young man who is turned into an ass after discovering the secrets of witchcraft, but is transformed back into human form by the goddess Isis) *798*

Augustine, St. [Aurelius Augustinus] (AD 354–430), Christian bishop and writer
Confessions (an autobiography) *585*

Aulus Gellius (ca. AD 125–128), Roman writer
Noctes Atticae (*The Attic Nights*: a miscellany of notes on philosophy, history, law, grammar, literary and textual criticism) *834*

Ausonius [Decimus Magnus Ausonius of Bordeaux] (fourth century AD), Roman poet
Epigrams 464, 638

Caecilius Statius (died 168 BC), Comic playwright from Milan
fabulae palliatae ("Greek" stories) *129*

Caesar [Caius Julius Caesar] (100–44 BC), general and political leader
De Bello Gallico (*On the Gallic War*: Caesar's campaigns in the provinces of Gaul, 58-49 BC) *839*

Calpurnius Siculus (mid-first century AD)
Eclogues (pastoral poems) *1010*

Cassiodorus [Magnus Aurelius Cassiodorus] (ca. AD 490–585), Senator
Variae (*Various Topics*: a collection of state papers on politics, culture, and ideology in the late Roman, Ostrogothic government) *450*

Celsus [Aurelius Cornelius Celsus] (first century AD), physician
De Remediis (*On Cures*) *200, 626*

Censorinus (third century AD), Roman grammarian
De Die Natali Liber ad Quintum Caerellium (*A Book on the Birthday for Quintus Caerellius*: an account on the origins of human life and divisions of time) *571*

Cicero see **Tullius**

Claudian (late fourth–early fifth centuries AD), Roman poet
In Rufinium (*Against Rufinus*: an invective against Rufinus, a Christian writer from Aquileia) *45, 444*

Columella [Lucius Junius Moderatus Columella] (fl. AD 50), writer on farming
De Re Rustica (*On Rustic Matters*: an extensive, systematic agricultural manual) *177*
Consolatio ad Liviam (*Consolation for Livia*, wife of Augustus, on the death of her son Drusus in 9 BC, traditionally, but falsely ascribed to Ovid) *850*

Curtius Rufus [Quintus Curtius Rufus] (first–second centuries AD), Roman historian

History of Alexander the Great 15, 97, 579, 622, 1153, 1171

Diogenes Laertius (third century AD)
A compendium of lives and doctrines of ancient philosophers 216

Dionysius Cato (ca. fourth century AD)
Disticha de moribus ad filium (*Distiches on Morality for His Son:* A collection of moral maxims in hexameter couplets) 21, 124, 358, 545, 1122

Ennius [Quintus Ennius] (239–169 BC)
Annales (*Annals:* an annalistic verse history of Rome from the fall of Troy, surviving in fragments) 244, 511, 564, 1043, 1137

Horace [Quintus Horatius Flaccus] (65–8 BC), Roman poet
Ars Poetica (*The Art of Poetry*) 870, 920, 946
Epistulae (Conversational and lightly satirical literary letters) 43, 153, 372, 533, 609, 784, 793, 811, 983
Carmines (*Odes:* lyric poems) 103, 248, 657, 729, 913, 1033
Sermones (*Satires:* colloquial and conversational poems) 270, 350, 380, 425, 527, 843, 999, 1018, 1111

Jerome, St. [Eusebius Hieronymus] (ca. AD 347–420), biblical scholar
Ad Pelam (*A Letter to Pela*) 936
Adversus Luciferum (*Against Lucifer*) 515
Epistulae (*Collected Letters*) 512, 660
Epistulae ad Ephesios proemium (*The Preface of the Letter to the Ephesians*) 542

Justinian [Flavius Petrus Sabbatius Iustinianus] (AD 527–565), Eastern Roman emperor
Institutiones (*Institutes,* Book 3 of Justinian's codification of Roman law) 666

Juvenal [Decimus Iunius Iuvenalis] (fl. early second century AD), Roman satirist
Satires (a rhetorical and critical assessment of contemporary society) 14, 27, 170, 190, 319, 322, 392, 570, 664, 722, 731, 846, 874, 897, 947, 1017, 1162, 1181

Lampridius [Aelius Lampridius] (fourth century AD), Roman biographer, contributor to the *Scriptores Historiae Augustae:* Biographies of the later Roman emperors)
De Vita Alexandri Severi (*The Life of Alexander Severus:* emperor of Rome, 225–235 AD) 1096

Livy [Titus Livius] (59 BC–AD 17), Roman historian
Ab Urbe Condita Libri (*Books from the Foundation of the City:* covering Roman history from the origins of Rome to 9 BC) 349, 844, 849, 855, 1014, 1139, 1142

Lucan [Marcus Annaeus Lucanus] (AD 39–65), writer of historical epic poetry
Pharsalia (also known as *De Bello Civili:* on the Civil War, an epic account of the civil war between Julius Caesar and Pompey) 301, 393, 562, 903, 928, 1183

Lucretius [Titus Lucretius Carus] (ca. 94–55/51 BC), Roman Epicurean philosopher
De Rerum Natura (*On the Nature of the Universe:* an epic account of natural philosophy, religion and ethics from an Epicurean point of view) 1110

Lygdamus (born 43 BC), Roman poet
Elegies (formerly attributed to Tibullus) 592, 653, 862

Macrobius [Macrobius Ambrosius Theodosius] (late fourth century AD)
Saturnalia (set in context of celebration of Saturnalia at the winter solstice, dialogues on various topics including law, grammar, the calendar, philosophy, religion) 247, 727, 986, 1035

Manilius [Marcus Manilius] (late first century BC–early first century AD), Roman Stoic philosopher
Astronomica (astronomical writings whose scope include philosophy and political

ideology) *1126*

Martial [Marcus Valerius Martialis] (AD
38/41–101/104), writer of epigrams
Epigrammaton Libri XII (*Twelve Books of
Epigrams*) *207, 427, 481, 517, 523, 591, 1102*

Nepos, Cornelius (ca. 110–24 BC), Roman
biographer
Atticus (Titus Pomponius Atticus, close
friend of M. Tullius Cicero, born 110 BC)
494
Epaminondas (Theban general, died 326
BC) *119*
Eumenes (of Cardia, secretary of Philip II
and Alexander the Great, 361–316 BC) *1036*
Timoleon (military leader who defeated
Carthage and expelled tyrants from Sicily
and Syracuse, fourth century BC) *610*

Ovid [Publius Ovidius Naso] (ca. 43 BC–AD
17), Roman poet, writer of love poetry
and mythology
Amores (*Love Elegies*) *197, 263, 551, 769,
1029, 1076*
Ars Amatoria (*The Art of Love*) *50, 84, 299,
344, 365, 538, 768, 782, 878, 926, 1007*
Epistulae Ex Ponto (*Letters from Pontus:*
written in exile) *19, 189, 357, 363, 856, 878,
926, 1007*
Fasti (*The Calendar:* an aetiology of Roman
cultic practices) *474, 805, 1074*
Heroides (*Heroines:* Letters from mythical
heroines to absent husbands or lovers) *56,
625*
Medicamina Faciei (*Cosmetics for the Female
Face*) *1186*
Metamorphoses (*Transformations:* a collection of stories from classical mythology)
*147, 351, 359, 606, 726, 820, 868, 939, 988,
1071, 1147*
Remedia Amoris (*The Remedy for Love*) *104,
307, 1097*
Tristia (*Sorrows:* written in exile at Pontus)

*290, 302, 462, 493, 673, 747, 813, 985, 1000,
1040, 1052, 1080*

Persius [Aulus Persius Flaccus] (AD 34–62),
Roman satirical poet
Satires 20

Petronius [Petronius Arbiter] (died AD 66),
Roman satirist
Satyrica (*The Satyrica:* a picaresque, mock
epic whose central characters are
unheroic) *42, 312, 437, 439, 443, 502, 532,
547, 698, 756, 783, 786, 885, 965, 1031*

Phaedrus [Gaius Iulius Phaedrus, or Phaeder]
(ca. 15 BC–ca. AD 50), writer of fables
Improbi iocos Phaedri (*Jokes of the
Mischievous Phaedrus*) *215, 670, 810, 827*

Plautus [Titus Maccius Plautus] (ca. 205–184
BC), Latin comic poet, many titles refer to
the name of a primary character
Amphitruo 654
Asinaria (*The Donkey Driver*) *714, 1152*
Aulularia (*The Money Jar*) *100*
Captivi (*The Captives*) *296, 475, 775, 723*
Curculio (*The Weevil*) *483, 505*
Epidicus 889
Menaechmi (A comedy of errors; identical
twins are separated at birth) *1046*
Mercator (*The Merchant*) *259, 405, 663*
Miles Gloriosus (*The Arrogant Soldier*) *388,
1156*
Mostellaria (*The Haunted House*) *127*
Persa (*The Persian*) *484, 643*
Poenulus (*The Little Carthaginian*) *235, 683,
1161*
Pseudolus (a crafty slave) *553, 720, 738*
Stichus 504, 1154
Truculentus (*The Aggressive Man*) *1022*

Pliny the Elder [Gaius Plinius Secundus] (AD
23/4–79), Roman natural historian
Naturalis Historia (*The Natural History:* a
compendious encyclopedia of contemporary Roman science) *471, 900, 916*